AIRFIX
magazine guide 13

The French Foreign Legion

Martin Windrow

Patrick Stephens Ltd
in association with Airfix Products Ltd

First published — 1976

ISBN 0 85059 224 0

Cover design by Tim McPhee

Text set in 8 on 9 pt Helvetica Medium by Blackfriars Press Limited, Leicester.
Printed on Fineblade cartridge 90 gsm and bound by the Garden City Press, Letchworth, Herts.
Published by Patrick Stephens Limited, Bar Hill, Cambridge, CB3 8EL, in association with Airfix Products Limited, London SW18.

Don't forget these other Airfix Magazine Guides!

Contents

Editor's Introduction 4
one   **The old Legion**   5
two   **The Crimea and Italy**   14
three   **Mexico**   19
four   **France and Africa 1867-1914**   25
five   **Tonkin, Dahomey and Madagascar**   33
six   **World War 1**   37
seven   **Between the wars**   40
eight   **World War 2**   47
nine   **Indo-China 1946-1954**   53
ten   **The last twenty years**   61

Editor's introduction

One of history's toughest and most respected fighting forces, the French Foreign Legion, has perhaps attracted more than its fair share of myth and legend, but has also covered itself in justly deserved glory.

First formed in 1831 for service in France's new colonial ventures, the Legion has seen action all over the world, from North Africa to Mexico and the Far East. Its most famous battles — Camerone, Bir Hakeim and Dien Bien Phu — are household names, while its képi and uniform are familiar to every schoolboy.

From its earliest days as virtually an armed rabble used principally for manual labour, the Legion gradually established itself as a rough, tough and thoroughly reliable military force, which successive French governments over the years have used as a 'fire brigade' wherever the fighting is dirtiest and hottest.

In this book, Martin Windrow — one of the world's foremost students of the Legion's history — traces its development from its earliest days fighting in Algeria in the 1830s and 40s, through the Crimean and Italian campaigns of the 1850s, the abortive Mexican venture in the 1860s, the Franco-Prussian War, its actions in North Africa and the Far East during the last quarter of the 19th Century and the first years of the 20th, through World War 1 and back to North Africa and Syria between the wars, into World War 2 and the postwar disasters in Indo-China, and right up to date.

As well as outlining its campaigns, its epic marches and heroic stands, he also describes its organisation and uniforms, and provides numerous hints for figure modellers wishing to depict légionnaires of any period — an ideal subject for a theme collection.

For anyone wishing to learn the truth about the Legion (rather than the glamour of romantic fiction), and for anyone assembling the Airfix Collectors Series kit of a légionnaire, this book is essential reading.

BRUCE QUARRIE

one

The old Legion

Foreign soldiers were no novelty in the armies of France long before the formation of the French Foreign Legion in 1831. The Valois kings had had their Scots guard, the Bourbons their regiments of Germans, Englishmen and Irishmen, and their famous Swiss, who fell defending Louis XVI from the Paris mob in the French Revolution. Napoleon, of course, made great use of foreign soldiers. France alone could

April 30 — Aubagne. An officer, escorted by a party of NCOs with unit fanions flying from their rifles, approaches the Legion's monument to its dead carrying the casket which contains Captain Danjou's hand (E.C.P. Armees).

not supply the manpower he needed for his ambitious campaigns. Defeated enemies pressed into French service, and countries swallowed by France's expansion under the First Empire, all provided regiments for his armies, and there were more foreigners than Frenchmen in the army Napoleon led into Russia in 1812. There had been a move to raise several foreign regiments for his last army during the Hundred Days of 1815, but in the event only one unit of Swiss could be organised in time to play a part in the Waterloo campaign. The restored Bourbon monarchy raised a regiment of foreign volunteers, mostly Germans, called the Regiment of Hohenlohe. This was disbanded on January 5 1831, and was the immediate ancestor of the Legion.

The idea of forming the Legion, specifically for service outside France itself, was attributed to the Minister of War, the wily old Marshal Soult, who had served with such distinction — but without many moral principles — under the great Napoleon. The king of France, Louis-Philippe, had only recently come to the throne and was threatened by a volatile political situation. There were large numbers of disgruntled ex-soldiers in the streets, ripe for trouble — and with the political conditions as they were, it was clear that someone might soon find employment for them to the disadvantage of the monarchy. Also, France had recently embarked on her first major colonial adventure — the invasion of Algeria. After a successful beginning this campaign was bogging down in indecisive but costly skirmishing, and casualties in this mismanaged campaign were causing much criticism in France. The plan for forming the Legion had the double advantage of removing the rowdies from the streets and packing them off where they could do no harm, and of providing cannon-fodder for Algeria which would attract no great political sympathy in France.

On March 9 1831 a law was passed authorising the raising of units of foreigners and natives both inside

Two views of model by author of Legion Voltigeur in the uniform worn on the foundation of the corps. The blue coat is lined and piped red, the trousers are red, and the shako is black with gold furniture and a red band. The epaulettes and pompon are in the yellow of the Voltigeur (or light) company. The model was a conversion using parts of two Series 77 metal castings, a French Napoleonic line Voltigeur and a British infantryman of the same period. The sword may have been the 1831 'coupe-chou' type, shaped like a Roman gladius — there is controversy over this, since the Legion was haphazardly equipped from various armouries in 1831 and may have received the old sabre-briquet shown here. The blue and white ticken roll contains the greatcoat. Note the yellow bugle-horns on the turn-backs.

France and in the overseas territories; and the following day the royal ordinance was signed which brought the Legion into being. The *Légion Etrangère* was to be organised into battalions of the same size as those of the French infantry of the line — ie eight companies of 112 men each — but was to have no flank companies — ie the company of grenadiers and the company of voltigeurs which, with six companies of fusiliers, made up the normal battalion. Men between 18 and 40 were eligible to enlist voluntarily for at least three years or at most five years, and apart from being in good health and at least five feet tall, there were no rigid conditions of entry. Lip-service was paid to the principle that each volunteer should present certificates of birth, good conduct and health, but it was clear that these would not be insisted upon. The units of the new formation were to be composed of men of the same nationality. Some days later a second, hurried instruction was issued forbidding entry to Frenchmen, Swiss, or married men without special authorisation. This was not effective — Frenchmen simply enlisted as Belgians. It was largely in order to allow the authorities to refuse some of the really hard cases from French jails which local councils were gleefully shipping into the recruiting depots, to get rid of them one way or another!

The formation of the Legion cannot be called efficient. The first depot was established at Langres, and others at Auxerre and Agen. Ex-soldiers, transients, drifters of every type, criminals on the run, romantic boys, old drunkards and diseased

French Foreign Legion

Model by author, from Airfix 95th Rifleman and Imperial Guard Grenadier kits, of a Legion Grenadier company trumpeter of the early 1830s. He wears the same coat as the Voltigeur illustrated on a previous page, but with the tricolour musician's lace around collar and cuffs: this white lace has a criss-cross pattern of blue lines with red squares in the centre. The epaulettes are red and the coat has a red grenade on each turnback. The cap has a brown leather flap at the rear; and note the carbine, carried by trumpeters.

derelicts rubbed shoulders with gullible would-be colonists who had been promised land in Algeria if they signed on. In several batches this rabble was shipped to Algiers, where the French held a narrow coastal strip around the main ports, and dumped on the quays without proper officers, uniforms, or much idea what they were doing there at all. A tough Swiss veteran, Colonel Stoffel, was appointed to whip them into shape. It was no easy task, and he had to resort to pretty robust disciplinary methods; the rabble was almost uncontrollable, and enjoyed beating up officers. Gradually, under his steely gaze, a sort of brigade emerged. By giving the few reliable ex-NCOs of the Swiss and Hohenlohe regiments their head, Stoffel created by July 1831 the 1st Battalion (Swiss and Hohenlohe veterans), the 2nd and 3rd Battalions (Swiss and German volunteers), the 4th Battalion (Spaniards) and the 5th Battalion (Sardinians and Italians). In

1833 and 1834 the 6th (Belgians and Dutch) and 7th (Poles) completed their formation in Algeria, and from the start a Polish company was attached to each of the other battalions.

This division into national battalions had the merit of allowing some sort of order to be imposed by using the minimum of interpreters, but it had serious disadvantages too. The prejudices and feuds of the outside world were carried on in the camps round Algiers, and for a long time légionnaires fought each other more fiercely than the Arabs. By the beginning of 1832 the boots and musket-butts of the NCOs had tamed them to a point where they could commence their duties, although for a long time the despised Legion was considered as fit only to wield shovels as a pioneer corps. In January the 1st, 2nd, 3rd and 5th Battalions were installed around Algiers, the 4th at Oran, and the partly formed 6th at Bône.

First blood

French policy towards Algeria was confused in these years. The invasion had no long-term strategic objective, and a decision to occupy and rule the whole of North Africa was far in the future. There was no proper local power-structure to negotiate with or defeat, but only a mass of tribes who happily raided the fringes of the narrow French-held corridor without reference to any central leadership. French operations were therefore reduced to short-term tactical expedients. One operation which seemed very expedient was the burning out of a hornet's nest of El Ouffia Arabs at a place called Maison Carrée. French labour gangs building roads and blockhouses in the area were frequently attacked or induced to desert by these gentry. On April 27 a line battalion, some 300 Chasseurs d'Afrique and a force from the 3rd Battalion of the Legion were sent in to attack the complex of buildings sheltering these Arabs, and succeeded in short order. The légionnaires were left as garrison after the subsequent counter-attack was repulsed.

A series of skirmishes followed during 1832 and 1833, against local Arabs and the followers of the Emir of Mascara, Abd'el Kader, who was emerging as the dominant native leader. The Legion battalions acquitted themselves well, took casualties and inflicted them, and under the pressure of events began to settle down as proper soldiers — although still regarded with scorn by the French military establishment. The Spaniards of the 4th Battalion, many of them ex-guerrillas, founded a particularly enviable reputation for broken-country fighting.

In June 1832 Stoffel was briefly replaced by Colonel Combe, who brought the Legion its first flag; he in his turn was soon followed by Colonel Bernelle. After battles at Arzew and Mostaganem the Legion had a quieter time until 1835; the muddled French policy involved trying to make terms with Kader, but he used the respite to regroup. In 1834 the 4th Battalion was

Drawings by Job of various headgears employed by French troops in Algeria when the unsuitability of the heavy felt and leather shako became obvious — the lower sketch shows the type finally adopted by most of the army (National Army Museum).

disbanded — the Spaniards were needed at home.

In 1835 Kader felt confident enough to make an attempt on Tlemcen. He by-passed the town and came up against a hastily-mounted French punitive column in the pass of Moulay Ishmael on June 26; it included the Italian 5th and Polish 7th Battalions of the Legion. In a confused and confined action the Poles held off the main attack and the Italians screened the flanks of the column while the cumbersome waggons were turned and a retreat began. Two officers were

French Foreign Legion

killed, one from each battalion, and an unknown number of légionnaires (Legion casualties were not officially announced, as an article of policy, for many years). The force pulled back towards Oran, and was ambushed again on the Macta salt-marsh two days later. This time the Arabs managed to break the column into groups, reached and butchered the wounded, and put to flight certain elements of the force — but not the légionnaires, who fought with distinction and covered the eventual withdrawal. A junior officer named Bazaine, wounded and mentioned in despatches in this, his first battle, would make himself a considerable name at the head of légionnaires in years to come.

In 1835, in an act of political cynicism, the Foreign Legion was handed over in its entirety to Spain. Its true worth was not yet appreciated in Paris; and as France had a commitment to support Queen Isabella of Spain against the revolution led by her uncle Don Carlos, it was felt that this rabble of foreigners was the most easily spared unit. The légionnaires and their officers were not lent, but actually signed over to Spain, and very inadequate precautions were taken to see that they would be properly treated — there was ambiguity about responsibility for their supply and payment, not areas in which Spanish authorities had an impressive record.

The hand-over was officially signed in June 1835, and the military orphans landed at Tarragona on August 17 — 123 officers and 4,021 men, less those who had died of disease on the transports. The battalions were split up and dispersed companies saw action against irregulars in Catalonia for some months. The advance of the royal forces the next winter involved the Legion in much hardship in the Pamplona area. On April 26 1836 the Legion distinguished itself against odds at Tirapegui, and later it added to its lustre at Zubiri. At the end of the year Colonel Bernelle, whose constant complaints about the neglect of his command were becoming irritating,

was replaced. By the time Colonel Conrad took over his command it had shrunk to three small battalions, ragged, hungry and disheartened.

In March 1937 the Legion operated in Aragon, and on June 2 at the bloody battle of Barbastro it was virtually wiped out and Conrad was killed. The Carlist unit opposite the Legion was itself a foreign volunteer formation, and many men in the ranks recognised old friends and enemies through the smoke of battle; in a surprising display of savagery the two volunteer units fought to a standstill, giving no quarter. (The Carlist War was as brutal, at all times, as any civil war in history, and the Spaniards made a habit of shooting wounded and prisoners.)

The few survivors of the Legion were left to rot at Pamplona, officially neglected — indeed, ignored — now that their usefulness was over. The officers who remained showed great devotion to their starving, freezing scarecrows, but it was December 1838 before the 500-strong rump of the Legion was disbanded. Amazingly, large numbers of these men elected to return to Algeria and enlist in the reborn Legion.

The new Legion

The removal of 4,000 experienced fighters from the French army in Algeria had left a serious gap, and in December 1835 another royal ordinance was signed creating a second Legion. At first recruits were sent off to Spain to fill the huge gaps left by casualties and desertion in the old Legion, but when it became clear that there was no future in this they were retained in France and trained. The first 800-strong battalion arrived in Algeria in January 1837, and a second battalion was formed in September of that year. A task-force battalion — *bataillon de marche* — was drawn from both these units for the expedition against the formidable Arab stronghold of Constantine that month. The walled city was built on a high rock, surrounded by ravines, in mountains swarming with tribesmen. Gen-

a *Legion Grenadier private in winter campaign dress of the late 1830s and early 1840s — the great period of Algerian conquest under Bugeaud. This figure is a composite of two contemporary watercolours which closely agree on all details. The* casquette d'Afrique *has a black oilcloth cover. The coat is dark steel grey, with red* ecussons *at the front edges of the collar, red Grenadier company epaulettes, and brass buttons. The garance-red trousers are worn loose over white gaiters and black shoes. A black waistbelt and neckstrap support a central cartridge pouch made out of old coat-cloth by the soldiers themselves. White straps support the natural cowhide pack and the blue and white ticken roll. The kidney-section tin canteen was often covered by the soldiers in old coat-cloth. The weapon is still a flintlock musket; usually it was carried with fixed bayonet, the scabbard being worn on the left side of the belt.* **b** *Legion Voltigeur private in the uniform and kit worn on Bugeaud's 'flying columns' in summertime during the early 1840s. This is taken directly from a Benigni painting and surviving items. The red* casquette *has a dark blue band and piping, blue loop to the brass button retaining the tricolour cockade, black peak, and white neck-cloth thrust under the rear edge. The white linen trousers are worn tucked into white canvas gaiters buttoning up the outside. The short, round-bottomed dark blue* veste *has red* ecussons *on the front edges of the standing collar, a single row of brass buttons, yellow Voltigeur company epaulettes, and red service chevrons on the left arm. The waistbelt and pouch neck-yoke are black, as is the pouch itself, now made from leather. The tin canteen is the only kit carried apart from the off-white (unbleached linen) horse-shoe roll. The socket bayonet is carried in a black scabbard with brass fittings, now on the right hip; the musket is still a flintlock* (Gerry Embleton).

b

The old Legion

eral Damremont's column was made up of zouaves, légionnaires, and line troops; it suffered great hardship during the advance from Bône through torrential rain, and during the siege and bombardment of the city from constant harassing attacks by the Kabylie tribesmen. Damremont and his chief of staff were killed before, on October 13 1837, the assault on the breaches went in. The Legion battalion distinguished itself, fighting its way through the maze of narrow alleys right across the city; Captain Saint Arnaud, another name destined to stay in the headlines, was at the head of one company. The Legion battalion remained as the garrison after the fighting was over; and in honour of their part in the victory the Legion battalions were granted permission to form *compagnies d'élite* — a grenadier and a voltigeur company in each battalion. In December 1837 a third battalion was formed, bringing effective strength of the Legion to just over 3,000. The 1st Battalion remained at Algiers, the others provided garrisons for Bône and Constantine. By late in 1839 four battalions were in being.

Abd'el-Kader was on the move once again, with an army of 6,000 and some 150 trained gunners. 1839 and 1840 were terrible years for the infant colony of Algeria — the Arabs swept across the settled plains, driving up to the very walls of the capital, and slaughtering all in their path. The 1st and 4th Battalions of the Legion fought in the advances on Medea and Milianah, two stiff battles which involved them in fighting off ambushes on the way to and from their objectives. The 4th Battalion remained in garrison at Milianah, and suffered hideous losses while besieged by the Arabs — between June 15 and October 5 some 460 out of 750 men died. Two battalions were also decimated by disease at Fondouk, losing nine officers and 207 men dead and 240 incapacitated. The 1st Battalion fought in a sharp action at Djidjelli in May 1839, losing their commander.

In December 1840 the Legion's recruiting figures were so healthy that it was divided into two regiments, each of three battalions, the 1st Regiment being stationed at Algiers and the 2nd at Bône. February 1841 saw the arrival as French Governor-General of the fiery General Bugeaud, who immediately instituted a new type of operation against the tribesmen. Instead of spreading his strength ineffectually over a vast number of small, vulnerable garrisons, Bugeaud concentrated on a few strong, strategic fortresses. From these a constant series of 'flying columns' fanned out through the disaffected areas, so that the Arabs could not tell from which direction they would be attacked next. The men were relieved of the more extreme burdens of European campaigning equipment, and provided with baggage mules to speed up their rate of march. These columns, composed of about three battalions of infantry, a couple of squadrons of Chasseurs d'Afrique, and a few mountain-guns, proved extremely effective, and the Legion played its full part in the raids — 'razzias' — which they mounted against dissident villages. By destroying the tribes' agricultural base and driving off their flocks Bugeaud forced them to move to his initiative, instead of the other way round. These operations occupied the years 1841-47, alternating with occasional large-scale manoeuvres aimed at trapping the elusive Abd'el-Kader.

In 1843 a major rising inspired by Kader was quickly cut up by the flying columns, and the Emir was forced to cross the border and take refuge in Morocco. The following year Bugeaud crossed the border and occupied the town of Oujda, and he would have marched on the Sultan's capital if not ordered to retreat by Paris. The Sultan interpreted this as a sign of weakness and brought his own troops to the Algerian border. On August 13 1844 Bugeaud, after a forced march by 8,000 French soldiers including the 1st Regiment of the Legion, launched a night attack on the huge Moroccan force on the Oued Isly. After fierce fighting he smashed the Sultan's

French Foreign Legion

army. The subsequent treaty gave him the right of hot pursuit of dissidents over the border, reducing still further Kader's chances of evading him indefinitely. He was finally captured and exiled in December 1847.

Other Legion battles during this period included Kolea, Mehab-Barboussen, and the two punishing attacks on the Zaatcha Oasis in 1849 — the latter were European-style battles, in that the Oasis was so well fortified and protected that it had to be reduced house by house with satchel-charges, like some desert Saragossa. Kabylia continued to simmer in the east, where the exiled Bey of Constantine was still active; the French were unable to penetrate the mountain heartland of Kabylia for years, but the *compagnies d'élite* of the 2nd Regiment of the Legion distinguished themselves in the taking of M'Chounech ridge in 1844. In the early 1850s a particularly active tribe, the Beni Snassen, rose in Western Algeria, and both regiments were on active service for months.

Modelling the Legion: 1831-1850

When the Legion was first raised in 1831 it was uniformed like the rest of the French infantry. A tall black shako with a red top-band and a yellow metal plate showing the Gallic cock over a star was decorated with brass chin-scales and pompons in company colours — the exact sequence is not clear. The blue coat was cut straight at the front with long tails at the back, and piped with red. When *compagnies d'élite* were created in April 1832 these received the usual ornaments: red epaulettes for the grenadiers, yellow for the voltigeurs, and grenade and bugle-horn badges respectively on the tail turn-backs. Centre companies wore blue *contre-epaulettes* piped red, and red stars on the turnbacks. The trousers were red, the usual French cross-belts white; the steel grey greatcoat was rolled and carried on the pack in a cylinder of striped white and blue cloth.

This uniform was less than practical,

and the shako disappeared within a year. It was replaced by a number of home-made caps, the first being made by stiffening into a cylinder the blue *bonnet de police,* with red piping, originally issued as off-duty wear, and adding a peak. Before long a properly made cap, the *casquette d'Afrique,* was issued; it had a blue band and a red crown, piped blue, and in shape was very like the British shako of 1800-1812. The various types of home-made cap, and this stiff type, were worn simultaneously, the stiff type becoming universal in about 1840, when it received a cockade and a loop of braid on the front. In bad weather — in practice, whenever worn on campaign — it had a black oilskin cover and neck-flap.

The blue uniform coat was quickly discarded into store in favour of the short single-breasted *veste* of plain dark blue with trident-shaped red collar patches. The flank companies added their epaulettes to this simple garment, and the usual French NCO and long service stripes were applied to the sleeves. The red trousers were often replaced by light white linen trousers in summer, tucked into buttoned cloth gaiters on campaign. The steel grey greatcoat, with the same red collar patches as the *veste,* was the usual campaigning dress.

The illustrations which accompany this chapter show models and artist's impressions of these uniforms. The many kinds of 54 mm figure depicting French Napoleonic infantry can be modified to resemble the 1831 uniform. The model bugler of 1835 wears a stiff *casquette d'Afrique,* simply made from an Airfix Rifleman's shako; his body is made by filing and filling the front of a Rifleman's torso, with the outer buttons trimmed away, until it marries with the rear torso and coat-tails of an Airfix Grenadier of the Imperial Guard. Arms and legs come from the two kits, to taste. The bugler's weapon was a carbine, and one from the Historex spares list is used here. The Rifleman kit could also be used to model the 1840 figure illustrated in the line artwork.

two

The Crimea and Italy

French officers in the Crimea; note the style of képis and epaulettes (National Army Museum).

In 1854 the Legion was ordered to provide two regiments of two battalions each for the Army of the Orient, embarking for the Crimean War. It seems that a single battalion of the 1st Regiment remained in Algeria, and the 3rd Battalion of the 2nd Regiment formed a depot at Bastia in Corsica. The four remaining battalions formed the 2nd Brigade of the 5th Division; the two regiments were commanded by Colonels Bazaine and de Caprez respectively, and the brigade by General Carbuccia. The légionnaires sailed for Gallipoli in June, and suffered badly from the cholera epidemic which ravaged the armies. On arrival in the Crimea most of the Foreign Brigade was kept in the rear for second-line duties — it must be remembered that the Legion's reputation among the conventional units was still not high — but an élite battalion was formed of the grenadier and voltigeur companies and posted to Canrobert's division. It fought, with notable success and dash, at the battle of the Alma on September 20 1854, and the remainder of the brigade was accordingly brought into the front line.

The two regiments fought throughout the siege of Sebastopol under appalling winter conditions, seeing action on numerous occasions; at Inkerman in November 1854 the 1st Battalion, 1st Regiment, lost 12 officers and nearly 150 men. They played a full part in the various assaults on Sebastopol in 1855, notably on May 1 (when Colonel Vienot, who had taken over the 1st Regiment when Bazaine

was promoted general and brigade commander, fell in a night attack); on June 7, at the White Works; and on September 8. After this successful attack Bazaine was appointed commandant of the captured city.

The Legion attracted a good deal of attention in the Crimea, with their Herculean drinking bouts, their enthusiastic foraging, their exotic slang, and their great fighting spirit. They were nicknamed 'Leather-bellies', on account of the big frontal cartridge pouches which they had invented in Africa and still wore on their belts; and also 'The Cabbage Brigade', from their foraging excesses. It is reported that an inspecting general — the fastidious Canrobert — was shocked rigid by discovering a glassy-eyed desert veteran parading in the snow with no boots and black-polished feet; he had sold the boots for liquor, and hoped the general wouldn't notice . . .

While the 'proper' Legion was enduring the snowy mud of the Crimea, at home in France the Emperor Napoleon III was tinkering about with the organisation of the army. In January 1855 he announced the formation of a '2nd Foreign Legion' composed of and officered by Swiss personnel exclusively and commanded by the Emperor's protegé, Colonel Oschenbein. It was to consist of two regiments of two battalions, plus a large battalion of tirailleurs uniformed and equipped in *Chasseur a pied* style. The new Legion was uniformed in green and red. Recruiting at the French depots was disappointing, however, and in April 1856 a less ambitious form was selected. The brigade returning from the Crimea was to be reorganised into a single regiment, designated (no doubt to their horror) '2nd Foreign Regiment', comprising three battalions and based on the famous depot at Sidi-bel-Abbès; while the Swiss were re-designated '1st Foreign Regiment', with two battalions and two companies of tirail-leurs, and based around Philippeville.

In April - June 1857 elements of both regiments participated in a major French drive which finally 'pacified' — on paper, at least — the rebellious heartland of Kabylia. Four converging columns totalling 35,000 men fought their way into the lunar landscape of the mountains, and two battalions of the 2nd Regiment did very well under the eyes of General MacMahon at Ischeriden on June 24 1857. A strongly defended ridge position had defied attacks by line troops; using their

Mule ambulance of the Crimean War. The Legion often fought in remote areas, and this basic form of casualty evacuation was still in use up to World War 1 and possibly later (National Army Museum).

Second Lieutenant, Legion Voltigeur company, in the parade uniform of the 1850s; from photographs, paintings, and uniform regulations. The képi is garance-red with a dark blue band and a squared black peak. There are gold buttons and chin-strap but no other insignia on the band. For this rank a line of gold lace ran round the top of the band, and a line rose vertically at front, back and sides. These joined a circle of gold lace running round the inner edge of the képi's slightly sunken top; a gold quatrefoil knot appeared in the centre of the top. The full-skirted single-breasted tunic is dark blue, piped with red around the yellow collar, down the front, and around the cuffs and three-quarters of the way around the cuff-slashes; the latter have three gold buttons, and there are nine on the front of the tunic. Gold bugle-horns indicate company affiliation; Grenadier officers wore gold grenades, Fusilier officers no collar insignia. On duty —and as this was the parade tunic, this meant at all times — the gilt gorget was worn; the company emblem appeared in the centre in silver. The gold epaulettes were worn as illustrated by this rank; lieutenants wore the fringed and unfringed epaulettes in the reverse positions, and captains fringed epaulettes on both shoulders. The same sequence was worn by majors, lieutenant-colonels and colonels, but with heavy bullion-twist fringes. The trousers, very full-cut but narrow at the ankle and strapping under the instep, are garance-red. The 1845 sabre has a gilt guard and gilt fittings on a black scabbard; the grip is black, the knot gold. The parade belt has a gold plate, and is of alternate red and gold longitudinal strips: from the top, gold-red-gold-red-gold-red-gold. The sabre suspenders are of the same pattern. The upper third of the sabre blade — nearest the guard — has an engraved foliage pattern and is of blued steel. White gloves are worn (Gerry Embleton).

expertise in broken-country fighting the légionnaires swarmed up the rocky slope under heavy fire, accepting casualties without firing a shot (and thus saving their cartridge 'up the spout' for the final assault, when it would do more good than if it had been fired up hill at enemies in cover), and finally taking the ridge with the bayonet in only half an hour. This exploit added to their reputation in the army, now growing brighter every year. The Swiss of the 1st Regiment then marched back to Sétif, and the 2nd to Sidi-bel-Abbès, for a period of

Study by Legion official artist Adjudant Rudy Burda of two Legion Pioniers — one of the Swiss '2nd Foreign Legion' of 1855, and one of today. The left hand figure wears a grass-green tunic with red epaulettes and distinctives, red trousers, and a red and green képi. The modern sapper wears khaki battledress with green, red-fringed epaulettes, a tan leather apron, and white gloves, gaiters, képi and axe handle. On his left arm is the green chevron of his rank — Soldat 1e Classe — and a dark blue diamond with green grenade and edging. On the right arm is a similar chevron and diamond, the latter bearing crossed green axes (Képi Blanc).

minor policing and construction work.

In 1859 Napoleon III launched his forces into war with Austria in Italy, in support of Sardinia. In April the still-weak 1st Regiment of the Legion was shipped to Corsica to recruit. The 2nd Regiment formed itself into four battalions, left one in depot at Sidi-bel-Abbès, and sailed with a strength of three battalions totalling 60 officers and 1,400 men for Italy. In May the two regiments were reunited at Genoa; together with the 2nd Zouaves they formed the 2nd Brigade (General Castagny) of General Espinasse's 2nd Division in MacMahon's 2nd Corps.

Fighting side by side in their green and blue uniforms, the two Foreign Regiments distinguished themselves at Magenta on June 4 1859. The 2nd Division of the 2nd Corps played a leading part in the victory, which was no credit to French leadership but achieved solely by the dash of the soldiers and junior officers. Losses during the advance through wooded and cultivated terrain were heavy, and Colonel Chabriere fell at the head of the 2nd Foreign Regiment; in all the Legion suffered 25 per cent casualties. After heavy house-to-house fighting in the town the Austrians withdrew. This was the occasion of MacMahon's famous remark — 'The Legion's there; this job's in the bag.'

On June 7 the Legion entered Milan, to an enthusiastic reception. The under-strength Swiss 1st Regiment remained in garrison, hoping to recruit there, while the 2nd, now led by Colonel Martinez, took part in the two-week pursuit of the Austrians which led to the bloody battle of Solferino on June 24 — another victory for the French soldier rather than for his generals. The 2nd Foreign Regiment then returned to Sidi-bel-Abbès, and the 1st to Bastia and, eventually, to Philippeville, Bougie and Constantine. At long last, in the winter of 1861-62, the Swiss experiment was abandoned. The remnants of the 1st Regiment were simply drafted into the ranks of the 2nd, which became the 'Foreign Regiment' — although still referred to as 'the Legion' by all true légionnaires.

Modelling the Legion: the 1850s

The campaign dress of the Legion in Algeria in the early 1850s comprised a square-peaked képi with a blue band, and a red crown and sides piped blue; a blue-grey double-breasted greatcoat with red patches on the low standing collar; and loose white trousers (red in winter) tucked into buttoned cloth spat-type gaiters of white or grey. The simple single-breasted dark blue *veste* with red collar patches was worn in summer. The black waist belt supported a leather cartridge pouch at the back, a bayonet scabbard on the left hip, and a large pouch of leather or cloth (see illustrations) on the front, the latter also supported by a strap from behind, passing round the neck. Elite companies wore their red or yellow epaulettes on the *veste,* and a grenadier with a blue cut-out grenade insignia on his red collar-patch has been illustrated. In 1852 centre companies ceased to wear *contre-epaulettes* of blue piped red, and received a fringed epaulette in green with a red crescent.

In 1856 the collar patches of the greatcoat became dark blue for the 2nd Foreign Regiment; apart from this, the only change between the Crimean and Italian campaign was the addition of a brass '2' to the band of the kepi. The uniforms of the '2nd Foreign Legion', later the 1st Foreign Regiment — the Swiss unit — were basically green; the details are complex, and since they never wore the tunic or shako in action this descriptions is confined to képi, *veste* and greatcoat of the line battalions: **Képi** Red sides and crown, grass-green band and piping, brass '1' after 1856; **Veste** Grass-green, with patches of same colour on collar, usual epaulettes; **Greatcoat** Steel grey, green collar patches, usual epaulettes; **Trousers** Red (white in summer); **Buttons** As for 2nd Regiment — yellow metal. NCO insignia, long service chevrons, and personal equipment all

Fine Benigni drawing of Legion NCO of the 1850s, in blue and red képi, steel grey coat with blue collar patches, red service chevrons and trousers, and characteristic frontal cartridge pouch from which came the nickname 'Leather-Bellies' (Képi Blanc).

followed the convention of the 2nd Regiment. In October 1859 the uniform was replaced by one identical to that of the 2nd Regiment, into which the Swiss were absorbed two years later.

The uniform of this period can best be modelled by simple modification of Stadden 54 mm castings depicting French troops of the Franco-Prussian War, 1870-71. The Swiss are not thought to have worn the large frontal ammunition pouch. Removal of the knapsack on the back of the 1870 castings, and the filing away of the strap supporting it at the shoulder, is the only structural modification required other than the addition of the pouch for the 2nd Regiment. At Magenta and Solferino the white summer trousers were worn. In the Crimean winter the red trousers would obviously have been worn, and the freezing légionnaires muffled themselves in blankets, goatskin jerkins, and anything else they could lay their hands on.

three

Mexico

The Legion's greatest epic took place far from its desert home in Algeria, in the course of a strange and rather pointless campaign on the other side of the world. In 1862 Napoleon III decided, for various complex reasons, to attempt to install a spare Austrian archduke, Maximilian, as Emperor of Mexico. Mexico already had a government, headed by President Juarez, and Napoleon's scheme, as soon became clear, could only hope to succeed if backed by a fairly massive invasion. This took place in due course, and a French army of 40,000 secured a corridor between the port of Vera Cruz and the strong Mexican city of Puebla well inland. No further advance could be made on Mexico City until Puebla fell, and this it declined to do for month after interminable month. It was at this point that the Legion came upon the scene.

In 1862 the *Régiment Etranger* of three battalions was based at Sidi-bel-Abbès under Colonel Jeanningros. The province of Oran was peaceful, and 5,000 civilians had moved into the area of what had once been a mud fort. The Legion was thunderstruck to be left out of the first French expedition, and the officers petitioned the Emperor. In January 1863 they received orders to prepare a *'régiment de marche'* of two battalions and an HQ company for service in Mexico, the 3rd Battalion and the depot alone remaining in Algeria. The légionnaires were jubilant at the thought of gold, exotic female company, and glory enough for all. Jeanningros led them

An officer of the Legion in Mexico, wearing the campaign tunic of zouave cut popular at that time. Of very dark blue, it had gold knots on the sleeves, and was usually worn open over a white shirt with ribbon tie, a waistcoat of dark blue, and a wide sash of red or blue. The very loose-cut trousers are red, the képi red and blue with gold rank piping (Via Milassin).

ashore, 2,000 strong, at Vera Cruz on March 28 1863. They quickly revised their opinions of Mexico.

There was no gold, no exotic female company, and worst of all, no glory. The Legion was posted in a string of small blockhouses along the route from Vera Cruz to the siege army at Puebla, to guard it against the incessant attacks of the guerrillas. They were firmly pinned in the coastal fever belt, a sweltering area of stagnant marshes and unhealthy jungle, with occasional bleached uplands. Desolation was complete; there was no entertainment, no fighting except irritating patrol actions with Mexican irregulars, and no loot. The men dropped like flies from disease, and the siege of Puebla dragged on.

On April 29 1863 Colonel Jeanningros, at Chiquihuite, received word that a convoy of siege material and bullion for the army at Puebla would leave a village down the track — Soledad — early the next day, marching in his direction by the route Palo Verde/Camaron/Paso Ancho/Paso del Macho/Chiquihuite. His duty was to send a patrol down the track to ensure the security of the route. He was unaware that only two kilometres off the track a Mexican colonel, Milan, was waiting with 500 regular cavalry, three battalions of regular infantry, and 300 mounted irregulars; but thanks to the efficient spy network of the enemy, Milan soon found out that a convoy was on its way up.

The duty company of the Legion was the 3rd of the 1st Battalion, down to 62 NCOs and men through disease; its only officer was laid low by fever, and the colonel's adjutant-major, Captain Jean Danjou, volunteered for the mission. Two other officers from the HQ company, 2nd Lts Maudet and Vilain, volunteered to accompany him. Captain Danjou was an experienced veteran of the Crimea and Italy; he had lost his left hand, and wore an articulated wooden replacement fixed to his wrist with a deep leather cuff. In the dawn of April 30 he led the 3rd Company off down the track. They were lightly equipped for this 24-hour mission, carrying their rations on mules and burdened only by their percussion rifle-muskets and 60 rounds per man. They wore big straw sombreros to protect them from the murderous sun on the march.

At first light they halted briefly at Paso del Macho, where the grenadier company of the 1st Battalion was stationed. Captain Saussier offered a platoon to Danjou, but he would not strip the little garrison of any men, and marched on alone. At about 7 am the 3rd Company halted for 'breakfast' — in the Legion, black coffee and bread — about a mile after passing through the deserted hamlet of Camaron (referred to hereafter by its French name, Camerone). The men poured out the contents of their canteens into the squad dixies, and the cooks brewed up. Minutes later the sentries sighted

Top *Captain Jean Danjou, photographed the year before his death at Camerone.* **Above** *2nd Lt Maudet, who led the last four légionnaires in the bayonet charge which won them immortality at Camerone (Via Milassin).*

strong groups of horsemen bearing down on them through the scrub.

The little force formed the Legion's

Fusilier, Mexico, 1863. The square-peaked képi has a white cover and neck-cloth, and a black chin-strap. A bright blue neck-stock is worn with a collarless white shirt. The short tunic is dark blue with red piping down the front and round the skirt, round the cuffs and three-quarters of the way round the cuff-slashes, and round the belt-loop on the left side only. The retaining loops for the epaulettes are blue with red piping each side. The collar is yellow, with red piping around the front and top. There are three brass buttons on each cuff and nine down the front. The epaulettes are entirely green except for red crescents; flank companies wore all-red and all-yellow epaulettes respectively, with a red grenade for the Grenadier company sewn to each side of the collar. The wide sash worn under the belt was either bright blue or red, apparently without regulation significance. The very full-cut trousers, often reinforced with leather, were garance-red; they were tucked into leather gaiters worn above white spatter-dashes. The gaiters were of light brown hide with thin black edging, lacing up the outside. A broad black belt with a plain brass plate and two brass slides supported a single large black pouch, worn at front or back to taste. The socket bayonet for the percussion rifle-musket hung in a black scabbard on the left hip. The only kit worn in the field was an off-white or fawn musette *(haversack) on the left side and a kidney-section tin canteen covered in dark blue-grey cloth on the right (Gerry Embleton).*

habitual hollow square and fell back, firing steadily, towards the cover of Camerone. In thick cactus scrub they were to some extent protected from the cavalry, but even so 16 men and — worse — the two mules with the rations and spare ammunition were separated from the company and shot down or captured. The remaining three officers and 46 men reached Camerone and threw themselves down behind cover.

The hamlet consisted of a derelict adobe inn or farmhouse in a

Four Legion types — a Greek, a Swiss-German, a Turk and a Spaniard —of the 'Légion du Papa', the old Legion of desert forts and blue greatcoats (Via Milassin).

courtyard surrounded by partly collapsed walls, with a few lean-to huts around the inside of the walls. But Mexican snipers had got there first and installed themselves in the main house, and it was under incessant point-blank fire that the légionnaires established themselves around a thin perimeter taking in one room of the farm, the walls, and the lean-to outhouses.

Suffering a steady trickle of casualties, they fought off several rushes by the cavalry outside, who had now dismounted and were surrounding the farm. The Mexicans were largely equipped with repeating carbines and rifles, in contrast to the single-shot muzzle-loaders of the Legion.

A surrender demand was made early in the action, but rejected by Danjou. Some time during the morning he is said to have made every man in the farm swear to him that they would not surrender. At about 11 am or noon, Danjou was killed by a bullet from a sniper in the scrubland, being struck in the chest and dying in seconds. Vilain took command. The courtyard in the blazing sun now contained many groaning wounded, tortured by thirst; to reach them one had to run the gauntlet of the snipers in the farm.

The sound of marching men raised the légionnaires' hopes agonisingly, but the newcomers were only Milan's 1,200 infantry reinforcements coming up to help. Charge after charge was beaten off, frequently at the point of the bayonet in the breaches of the battered walls; and one by one the defenders fell. Vilain died at about 2 pm, and Maudet took over, seizing a dead man's rifle and cartridges and rallying the little garrison.

The enemy fired the buildings, and smoke choked men already tormented by sun and thirst. The snipers now overlooked the whole perimeter, and the légionnaires moved at their peril. Still the Mexicans outside the walls fired, and charged, and fell back only to charge again.

By 5 pm Maudet had only 12 men left on their feet. He had rejected further surrender demands in strong terms, but a concentrated rush by the enemy drove the French right out of the farmhouse and confined them to a few of the miserable sheds in the courtyard, under fire at short range from all directions. Some time before 6 pm Maudet found himself with only four men, and each was down to his last cartridge. On his word of command they fired the last round; then, in a display of defiant courage which astonished the enemy, the five men charged with the bayonet into the front ranks of the Mexicans.

Maudet and one légionnaire fell at once; Colonel Milan prevented his men killing Corporal Maine and the other two (Privates Wenzel and

Constantin). In all 52 officers and men of the 3rd Company died in action or later of their wounds; one wounded man, the drummer, escaped by feigning death under a pile of corpses and, despite hideous wounds, lived to tell the story of the action to Jeanningros when he arrived on May 1 with a relief column. 12 prisoners, including Maine, were eventually handed over to the French under an exchange. The company had held off 2,000 men for 11 hours, inflicting some 300 fatal and about the same number of lesser casualties. The convoy, hearing gunfire, had turned back to safety.

Picking through the smoking rubble, Jeanningros found the battered wooden hand. This he kept in his baggage for the rest of the war, and took back to Sidi-bel-Abbès in 1867. There, the most sacred relic of the Legion and the symbol of final defiance in the face of hopeless odds, it rested in the Salle d'Honneur until the Legion moved its depot to Aubagne in the early 1960s. The hand of Danjou is still paraded before the légionnaires every April 30, and Camerone Day is a far more important occasion for the Legion than Christmas. The story of the battle is read aloud to every Legion unit, wherever they may be, as the climax of impressive ceremonial.

It would be dramatically satisfying if the Legion's involvement in Mexico had ended at Camerone, but unfortunately it didn't. The war, hopeless politically even though militarily promising once the energetic Bazaine took

over supreme command, dragged on for four years. The Legion played its full part in the depressing convoy escorts, outpost actions, ambushes and drives against the guerrillas. Bazaine conducted an able campaign against the main enemy army, forcing them back almost to the US border by an offensive planned on Algerian lines; but Maximilian failed to attract any serious local support, without which his throne could survive only as long as French bayonets surrounded it. This open-ended commitment was obviously more than France had bargained for. The USA, now at peace again after her civil war, was in no mood to tolerate European armies on the North American continent, and threatened to intervene on the side of Juarez.

The last major battle was another defeat for the Legion, but of a different kind. In February 1866 Chef de Bataillon Brian was based at Parras, in the bandit-haunted north, with four companies of the 2nd Battalion and some Mexican auxiliaries. He received word of a Juarist force nearby, and, disobeying orders, marched out with the bulk of his force to deal with them. Of the eight officers and 177 men who attacked the Juarists at Santa Isabel on March 1, only one returned. They walked into an ambush set by 1,500 Juarists, and were wiped out: only one officer and 81 men survived to be taken prisoner, and 40 of those died in captivity.

In February 1867 the Legion

embarked for home at Vera Cruz. The French army was being pulled out, and despite repeated advice Maximilian was staying on in the mad hope of success. He ended up against a wall shortly afterwards. For one dreadful moment it had been thought that the Legion was to be left as well, in a repetition of the Carlist War, but luckily for the honour of France this plan was hastily buried. In all the Mexican campaign cost the Legion 31 officers and 1,917 NCOs and men.

Modelling the Legion: Mexico 1863-67

In 1860 the Legion received a new uniform. A short tunic of dark blue was fastened by one row of nine buttons. The front, bottom edge and cuffs were piped red, with cuff details identical to the 1831 *habit*. The yellow collar was piped red, and for élite companies bore a red grenade or bugle-horn, in association with the usual epaulettes. Centre companies had plain collars. The very baggy red trousers were confined in fawn leather leggings (almost concealed by the pull-down of the trousers) above white buttoned 'spats' reaching to just above the ankle. The square-peaked képi, with white cover and neck-cloth, was worn in action; large local sombreros were used at other times.

Although officially suppressed, the plain dark blue *veste* was probably worn a lot in the field, with locally-made white trousers of less generous cut than the red issue type, and buttoned cloth gaiters. The long woollen body-belt, in blue or red, seems to have been worn outside the veste for the first time in this campaign. The big frontal pouch would have been worn by many men.

No proprietary casting is available at the time of writing, but an American manufacturer of 54 mm figures has announced his intention of producing one. The simpler campaign dress (the blue *veste* with external sash and white trousers, worn with either the sombrero or covered képi) should not be beyond the skill of experienced modellers working with Airfix and/or Historex 54 mm kit parts.

four

France and Africa 1867-1914

On returning from Mexico the Legion took up its old duties in Algeria, the three battalions being based at Mascara, Sidi-bel-Abbès and Saida. The next few years were not the best in the Legion's record. There was some scattered fighting against dissident tribes, but mostly the légionnaires were condemned to back-breaking construction work and monotonous duty in little desert forts. The calibre of the officers declined somewhat in peacetime, and the largely unsupervised senior NCOs sometimes abused their authority, giving rise to the horror-stories all too often found in exaggerated novels about the Legion. 1868 saw the end of *compagnies d'élite* throughout the French army; and in the same year a fourth battalion of the Legion was formed.

When France and Prussia came to open warfare after years of tension, in 1870, there were many foreigners in France who wished to offer their services to the Empire. In August it was decided that these volunteers should form a 5th Battalion of the Legion, formed at Tours, although the connection with the Legion proper was tenuous. It fought well at Bel-Air-les-Aides near Orleans, but was badly cut up at Bannier in the second week of October 1870. Simultaneously two of the four other battalions of the Legion (minus the German légionnaires, who remained in Algeria) arrived in France, and the 1st, 2nd and 5th Battalions served together thereafter in the 1st Brigade of the 2nd Division of the 15th Corps of the Army of the Loire, and subsequently in the Army of the East and the Army of Versailles. The légionnaires saw hard fighting at Cercottes and Chevilly, and at Besançon in January 1871. In May the regiment, 1,000 strong, was sent into the streets of Paris and took part in the fearful civil war against the Communards; and in mid-June it was shipped home again from Toulon, and marched back to its headquarters at Mascara.

The Prussian victory of 1870-71 had obviously encouraged the tribes of North Africa to revolt, and the 3rd and 4th Battalions had had hard fighting in Kabylia during the absence of their comrades. There were a series of

The courtyard of the Sidi-bel-Abbès depot, a great barracks designed and built entirely by légionnaires — as, indeed, was much of the town which surrounded it. The bedding is being aired in this picture — thus the bedsteads in the open air! (Via Milassin).

France and Africa 1867-1914

small but vicious actions on their return, notably against their old enemies on the Moroccan border, the Ouled Sidi Cheikh. By 1872 things had quietened down, with battalions posted at Mascara (HQ), Géryville, Sidi-bel-Abbès and Saida.

In 1875 the name of the formation, which had officially wavered between 'Légion Etrangère' and 'Régiment(s) Etranger(s)' depending upon current strength, was finally decided — the Légion it would be. Strength was fixed at four battalions of four companies each. In 1871 Colonel de Malaret had begun what would be a ten-year appointment as commander of the Legion, and during this period many of the abuses which had sprung up were curbed and a steadier atmosphere was achieved. There was very little serious fighting; the greater part of Algeria was pacified, and colonisation proceeded. Slowly the Legion, for lack of enemies, began to sink into the role of a labour corps. It had always been handy with a pick and shovel, and ready to turn its skill to any job that needed doing; now this self-sufficiency became a trap.

Below *Légionnaires in képis, sashes and shirtsleeve order on the drill square of Saida, the depot of the 2nd RE (Via Milassin).* **Bottom** *The column has reached its goal, and the General is explaining French policy to Arab chieftains, surrounded by his officers and backed by the bayonets of the Legion (Via Milassin).*

French Foreign Legion

As the 1880s opened the Legion was rescued from this gentle fate by a number of events. In 1881 Colonel de Negrier, one of the Legion's greatest commanders, took over. He formed a great affection for his hard-bitten rogues, and under his command life became both more exciting and more dignified for the common soldiers. Negrier wanted no slaves or labourers, he wanted soldiers — and he got them. He instituted the first mounted companies, the very successful experiment which enabled légionnaires to cover up to 50 kilometres a day over the roughest terrain. These units were equipped with one mule for each two men. The mule carried the packs; and one man rode while his mate marched at the stirrup, changing places every hour. These mounted companies became a legend within a legend, and the terror of rebellious tribes; they would turn up out of nowhere, and go yelling into the attack before the warriors were awake and out of their tents.

Another significant event in 1881 was a law allowing Frenchmen to enlist in the Legion for the first time; although many had done so before, now that it could be done openly it attracted many of the more adventurous and steady would-be soldiers.

In 1882 there was more trouble among the Ouled Sidi Cheikh, and in April there occurred a famous action at a place called Chott Tigri, near Haci-bel-Salem. A survey party escorted by two rifle companies and the mounted company of the Legion was attacked, while the column was dislocated by a sand-storm, by huge numbers of Arabs led by a noted chief named Bou-Amana. Their numbers can never be accurately settled, but there were somewhere between 800 and 1,500 horsemen and at least twice that number on foot. The Legion force totalled some 300, and was badly scattered. Three separate little forts of dead mules and baggage were pinned down by the charges of the tribesmen. After stiff fighting two managed to join up on a slight hillock but the mounted company was still cut off, a quarter of

a mile away, firing steadily under the command of an old légionnaire, as both officers and all the NCOs had been killed early in the action. The Arab charges went on for seven hours, and in the intervals the agonised defenders could see and hear comrades who had been dragged away in hand-to-hand fighting being tortured to death just out of rifle range of the squares. At last the Arabs seemed to lose heart after suffering several hundred casualties, and the two French squares joined up. With the wounded in the middle of the hollow formation they began a slow withdrawal to Gelloul, harassed all the way by sudden attacks. At last they met up with a relief column under Negrier, having lost two officers and 49 men dead and three officers and 28 men wounded. In early May two Legion battalions took part in extensive sweeps in search of Bou-Amana's band, but although the tribes were cowed the sheikh slipped safely over the Moroccan border into the traditional refuge of enemies of France.

In 1883-85 the Legion was heavily committed to the conquest of Indo-China (see next chapter), as North Africa entered a period of peace broken only by the occasional tribal squabble, easily quelled by the tireless mounted companies. In December 1884 the Legion was split once again into two regiments, and from this point on they will be referred to as the 1st and 2nd RE (Régiments Etrangères). The main garrisons were Sidi-bel-Abbès, Géryville, Saida and Tiaret. Each regiment mustered four battalions. In September 1883 the Legion's 1st Battalion had been ordered to Tonkin, and when the two regiments were separated this became the 1st Battalion, 1st RE. In December 1883 the Legion's 2nd Battalion followed suit, to become the 2nd Battalion, 1st RE. In November 1884 the Legion's 3rd and 4th Battalions were sent East, to become the 3rd and 4th Battalions, 2nd RE; by this time six battalions were in existence. During the 1890s and 1900s the Legion continued to send drafts out to Tonkin, replacing

Above *Colour party of the 1st RE, 1911. The men wear their tunics and white trousers.* **Below** *Contrasting shot of the 2nd RE colour party at the same period. The men wear red trousers and steel-grey greatcoats. The képi was always worn uncovered for formal occasions until 1939 (Via Milassin).*

French Foreign Legion

Suspiciously neat and quiet légion-naires pose in the reading room of the Saida depot. Most are in shirtsleeve order, covered képis, sashes, leather gaiters and boots (Via Milassin).

units or drafts returning to Africa. In 1899 each RE was raised to a strength of six battalions.

The same period saw the gradual expansion of the French rule south-wards into the true Sahara. The Legion played its part, particularly the mounted companies, in a series of small actions. In 1903 the 22nd Mounted Company of the 2nd RE was almost wiped out at El Moungar. The appointment of Colonel Lyautey to the command of Oran Province in October of that year brought to an end a period in which a certain lack of co-ordination was visible in French oper-ations, and within three years the desert was calm again as far as the Moroccan border. It was not to be long before the old refuge was opened up forever.

Morocco

Morocco had avoided French occu-pation by skilled diplomacy for years, but in 1906 France persuaded the other colonial powers, England and Spain, to give her a free hand. The folly of a weak Sultan in Fez played into French hands, and early in 1907 the town of Oujda just across the bor-der was occupied by a column includ-ing the mounted company of the 1st RE. The obvious next step of an advance on Fez was delayed; the terrain was a nightmare, and it was felt desirable that no very prolonged cam-paign be launched. Riots in Casa-blanca which threatened European lives gave the excuse for a landing at the port by forces including the 6th Battalion, 1st RE, and thereafter the French expanded from the coastal enclave into the interior of the coun-try. In September 1907 fierce tribal resistance led to the transfer of rein-forcements, including two battalions of the 2nd RE.

In the period of penetration, 1907-14, the battalions of the 1st RE oper-ated basically in Eastern Morocco, and those of the 2nd in Western Morocco. Apart from depots and minor policing units, most of the fight-ing strength of the Legion was concentrated either in Morocco or

Tonkin. Clashes during the first year of operations included actions at Taddert and Sidi Brahim, and October saw an attack on the Moroccan centre of Mediouna, some 1,000 légionnaires participating. For some reason the French withdrew after capturing the city without leaving a garrison, and the enemy promptly re-occupied it, to the acid amusement of the Press. General Drude took it a second time in January 1908, but was soon replaced by General d'Amade, who shortly thereafter took Settat. Early in 1908 there were fights on the Mellah river and at M'Karto, and after that resistance seemed to ease. Many Legion units were posted back to Algeria. They had made a great impression on the international Press during this campaign, with their superior marksmanship, their imperturbable advance under fire, and their cheerful improvisation and ingenious field-craft. Something of the romantic legend was already beginning to cling to them, thanks to the fevered brains of over-excited journalists.

Another of the periodic outbreaks of rebellion among the Beni Snassen

Two veteran légionnaires in full campaign kit, 1911. Note medals worn at all times, huge packs with tent-rolls and bivouac poles, and Lebel rifles (Via Milassin).

French Foreign Legion

Model by author of a veteran Légionnaire de 1e Classe in campaigning kit during the penetration of Morocco — a Series 77 casting with minor additions such as mug and firewood. The red chevrons indicate 15 years' service, the red bugle-horn below them a third class marksman award. The rolled sleeves of the capote *almost hide the single red diagonal stripe of a 1st Class Private.*

around Géryville occupied the Legion for a while, and in April 1908 a fierce fight at Menabha cost one company 120 casualties and would have turned into a massacre if the situation had not been saved by a traditional Legion bayonet charge. Another success, Beni Ouzien, broke the spirit of rebellion for a while. The mounted companies continued their patrols, and Morocco simmered.

In April 1911 riots in Fez again provided an excuse, and General Moinier led 35,000 men inland from Casablanca while General Toutee prepared another column at Oujda. A battalion of the Legion (1st Battalion, 2nd RE?) and the 3rd Mounted Company of the 2nd RE took part in Moinier's advance from Kenitra to Fez, and distinguished themselves; the column arrived at the capital late in May. Meanwhile, around Oujda, scattered fighting continued and increased, and any immediate

westwards advance was halted.

At Alouana on May 15 1911 the 22nd Company, 6th Battalion, 1st RE was badly cut up in an ambush, remembered in the Legion for the heroism of two légionnaires in particular. Surrounded, and mortally wounded, they were found to have removed the bolts from their Lebel rifles and hidden them under their bodies, so that after they eventually died the tribesmen could not make use of their guns.

By the Treaty of Fez in March 1912 Morocco passed under French 'protection', and the announcement stirred the tribes to new fury. The Legion was heavily engaged in the subsequent campaign, and 1913 saw many battles along the line Rabat-Fez and in the mountainous Tache de Taza. In May-June 1914 the long-awaited pincer movement established a corridor between Fez and Oujda, the légionnaires fought in both armies.

Modelling the Legion: Franco-Prussian War, and North Africa 1867-1914

The Stadden 54 mm castings of personnel of the French line, 1870-71, can easily be painted to resemble Foreign Legion troops of this period. During the war in France they wore the same uniforms as the line except for minor insignia. The képi bore a red five-pointed star on the blue band at the front. The greatcoat bore plain dark blue collar-patches, and all companies wore green epaulettes with red crescents. The battalion formed in France differed only in that buttons were of white metal instead of yellow, and the képi star was replaced by a white cloth '5'.

The same castings, slightly modified, can be painted as légionnaires in North Africa. In the mid-1870s the képi acquired a round peak and a red grenade badge on the band. From the early 1870s to 1884 the greatcoat bore red grenades on the collar, and after that the number of the regiment in dark blue, almost invisible against the dark blue-grey cloth. From 1872 the epaulettes were of green material, with both crescents and fringes red. During the late 1870s and 1880s the white-covered képi with a neck-cloth became popular, and remained so until World War 1. Sometimes it was pale khaki. White trousers were worn in the field in summer.

Pictures show many Legion units in Algeria and Morocco in the early years of the century on campaign in shirt-sleeve order; a coarse, loose shirt of white linen with a tab collar buttoning to the right, worn with white linen trousers, the blue sash of the Legion, black leather anklets, Lebel rifle equipment, and canteen and haversack slung on cross-straps. The képi often had its neck-cloth tucked up inside when not in use. White-covered tropical helmets of tall profile were worn instead of kepis under particularly punishing climates, notably in South Oran Province.

A Series 77 casting of a légionnaire in Morocco is available, and the new Airfix 54 mm kit depicts a légionnaire of this period.

five

Tonkin, Dahomey and Madagascar

In September 1883 General Negrier was posted from the Legion to command one of the elements of the French invasion force then being sent to Indo-China. France had been extending her influence here for a century, and now intended to settle a festering situation by outright occupation. Her enemies were the 'Black Flags', Chinese irregulars sent down from Yunnan by the Empress but only nominally under her control. Now about 25,000 strong, they possessed a fair proportion of modern weapons and some elderly artillery, and although weak in set-piece actions and poor at co-ordinating the efforts of the different marauder bands, they were past masters of jungle ambushes and swift raids.

A French-Swiss légionnaire in the tropical helmet worn both in Indo-China and in the desert wastes of South Oran province (Via Milassin).

Negrier specifically asked for a detachment of légionnaires to join the Turcos and 'Marsouins' of his advance guard; he had formed an affection for his leathery old soaks, and knew their worth in a hard campaign. In November the 1st Battalion of the Legion marched ashore in Haiphong, and moved up to Hanoi where a force was being assembled to assault the Black Flag fortresses, Son Tay and Bac Ninh. Son Tay, an old Chinese brick fort some 30 miles away on the Claire river, was attacked on December 16 by 5,000 légionnaires, line troops and marine infantry. After stiff fighting a Legion sergeant named Minnaert leapt over the secondary line of defences, and with a cheer the légionnaires followed him with the bayonet. An hour later all was quiet and the fort flew the tricolour.

In February 1884 the 2nd Battalion of the Legion arrived at Haiphong; and both battalions took part in the capture of Bac Ninh in March, one acting as a flanking pivot for the advance and the other leading the storming party. After tough fighting through a line of barricaded villages the fort itself fell; inside the French found large numbers of repeating rifles and some brand new German artillery pieces.

The Legion battalions then embarked on an exhausting period of patrol operations, the 1st around Tuyen Quang, the key post on the river Claire then still in enemy hands, and the 2nd around Hung-Hoa. Both units became adept at jungle fighting and usually provided the 'point' when on column; but this kind of nerve-racking work in the swamps took a heavy toll by wounds and fever.

Eventually Tuyen Quang fell into French hands, and was garrisoned by two companies of the 1st Battalion and two companies of line troops, a total of about 390 men. For months the Black Flags filtered through the jungles, building up their strength around the isolated fort, but as they considered the garrison well provisioned the High Command did not worry unduly. In January 1885, with 20,000 men in position, the Chinese attacked. The assault was beaten off with difficulty, and the little garrison began a harrowing ordeal which lasted until the first week of March. The Chinese sapped and mined energetically and kept up a constant barrage of artillery and small-arms fire. Large sections of the walls were blown up with mines, and mass attacks by infantry pressed in on the breaches. The dwindling garrison had a desperate time trying to spread themselves over their long perimeters, and on many occasions disaster was only avoided by hand-to-hand fighting in the breaches. By the time Negrier's relief column made contact with the southern edge of the siege force on March 2 more than 50 yards of the wall had been blown down and the garrison had suffered 56 fatalities and 208 wounded.

Early in 1885 the 3rd and 4th Battalions of the Legion arrived in Indo-China, the 4th after a hard little campaign on Formosa between January and June. Sporadic outpost actions and ambushes carried on for ten years, but there were no pitched battles of note, and the last significant clash with the Black Flags took place in 1895. The four battalions of légionnaires remained in a chain of small garrisons, settling down to a relatively quiet life which lasted until 1941. The 1st Battalion of the 1st RE went back to Algeria in 1897; and two battalions were posted out to Tonkin temporarily in 1900-01 to take the strain when drafts of colonial infantry were shipped out for the Chinese expedition. In 1903 the garrison was raised from three to four battalions again, the 5th/2nd RE coming out to join the 2nd/1st RE, the 4th/1st RE and the 3rd/2nd RE. After some shuffling of titles which further confused the issue, the garrison was reduced to three units again in 1907.

Dahomey and the Sudan

In the summer and autumn of 1892 a small but dramatic campaign occupied a *bataillon de marche* under Chef de Bataillon Faurax, in a pestilential little country on the west coast of Africa. An expeditionary force under Colonel Dodd landed in August 1892 at Cotonou, a port of Dahomey, the small kingdom on the Bight of Benin between Togo, Nigeria and Niger. This evil strip of jungle running north on

French Foreign Legion

each side of the Oueme river was ruled by one King Behanzin, who inhabited a skull-bedecked hut well up-country at Abomey, protected by 150 miles of fever-ridden swamp-jungle and 10,000 warriors — among them, an extraordinary regiment of young women armed with pangas and Winchester repeaters. For some time the slaver king had been annoying the French by his treatment of their traders and his contempt for treaties, and the excuse for clearing out this pocket of barbarism was provided by his slaving and his enormous festivals of human sacrifice, which were lurid even by African standards.

The Legion duly provided a battalion drawn from the two regiments in North Africa, and late in August the column started up-country, the légionnaires as usual providing the

Légionnaire in winter campaign dress, Tonkin, 1885. Legion uniform stocks ran out quickly in Tonkin, and the replacement clothing came from Infanterie de Marine *stores; this figure is based on surviving items in the Legion's museum. The white colonial helmet is covered with a roughly-stitched sleeve of dark blue, black, grey or brown cloth. The midnight-blue double-breasted tunic has no insignia apart from Legion brass buttons; it is worn over a white shirt with a low standing collar. The Legion's sash of deep royal blue is worn round the waist under the belt. The trousers are of light blue flannel — white linen in summer; the gaiters are white canvas, buttoning up the outside. Belt and pouch are black, as is the locally-made chest-pouch fixed with a neck-yoke and a strap passing round the back. This so-called 'Negrier pouch' was made by the men themselves from available materials, and white canvas models are often illustrated; the one in the Legion museum appears to be made of black oilcloth, or thin leather. A white haversack is slung on the left hip, over the hilt of the bayonet for the Le Gras bolt-action single-shot rifle, whose barrel, furniture and action are of bright metal* (Gerry Embleton).

advance guard. Each night the force formed square, but even so it was nearly overrun on September 19 by a dawn attack which caused some confusion. The natives, supported by snipers in the trees and led by the fearless Amazons, broke into the French camp, and the bayonet-charge which eventually expelled them cost the life of Faurax. Some 800 Africans were killed in this battle of Dogba, which lasted five hours and involved some 4,000 natives and about 2,300 Europeans.

Harassed by further delaying attacks on October 4, 14 and 20, during which the Amazons proved to be by far the best troops in Behanzin's army, the column reached Kana on November 4, and took the abandoned capital of Abomey a few days later. The Legion was shipped back to Algeria in due course, after suffering some 40 dead in action.

In September 1892-June 1893, and again in February 1894-January 1895, mule-mounted *compagnies de marche* of the Legion were sent to the Sudan for operations against troublesome Arab slavers in the area through which France then intended to build a transcontinental railway. Volunteers were picked for their youth and fitness. Little is known about their operations, except that they covered the extraordinary total of 12,000 miles through Guinea, Senegal, Volta and the Sudan, and that they had considerable success. The company suffered many wounded in 1894 at the taking of the village of a chief named Alikari.

Madagascar

In April 1895 the French landed a force at Majunga on the west coast of Madagascar, ostensibly to aid the Sakalava tribe against the dominant Hova monarchy but in fact with more complex motives. The capital of Tananarive was far to the south-east in the central mountains, and the best approaches to it were on the east side of the island — but so were the best defences. The Hova army was large, and because the Queen had hired a number of mercenary European officers and was known to have modern artillery, it was felt wiser for the French to come in by 'the back door'. This decision was founded on a monumental ignorance of local conditions. The terrain and climate were hideous, and the expeditionary force suffered very heavy casualties from disease, which they were not equipped to handle.

The spearhead of the French column, not surprisingly, was made up of légionnaires of a *bataillon de marche* attached to General Metzinger's brigade. The French authorities, disdainful though they still pretended to be of this roughneck regiment, had clearly learned the lesson of past campaigns; whenever there was particularly dirty or unrewarding or dangerous work to be done, the Legion would be first in the advance, last in the retreat.

It was noticeable that the Legion's casualties from disease were fewer than those of line troops; they were tougher, hardened to bad climates and bad water, their sanitary discipline was better, and they did not mingle with other units in camp. Even so, they lost 266 men dead of disease and heat-stroke and only five in combat — though those five represented five-sevenths of the total French combat losses in the campaign!

The Legion bore more than its share of fighting and track-building during the advance, which did not reach the capital until mid-September. There were actions with the Hovas at Naked Heights, Suburbieville, Andriba and Tsinaindry, but these were not large affairs; the Hovas tended to run at first contact, despite the efforts of their European advisers and the modern guns, both of which turned out to be real. The Legion provided a new battalion for Madagascar in 1896, which stayed until 1904 on pacification duties.

Modelling the Legion: Tonkin, Dahomey and Madagascar

When the Legion first sent a battalion to Haiphong, it was dressed as for Morocco — covered képi with neckcloth, greatcoat, *veste*, red or white trousers, blue sash worn outside the coat. The climate soon rendered this useless, but stocks of Legion clothing were not available, so the légionnaires were kitted out with Marine Infantry uniforms. These consisted of a dark blue double-breasted tunic with a standing collar, pale blue or white summer trousers, calf-length white buttoned 'spat' gaiters, and a white colonial helmet. In time the Legion covered the helmet with darker local cloth of black, blue, or grey; they removed the 'Marsouin' anchor insignia from the tunics, and added their blue sash to the ensemble. In hot weather or in the field they usually stuck to shirtsleeve order. A feature of the campaign was the 'Negrier' pouch, a long narrow reserve ammunition pouch carried across the chest, fastened with varying numbers of buttons.

In Dahomey the colonial helmet was worn with white trousers bloused at the ankle, and a khaki, collarless, single-breasted jacket. In Madagascar shirtsleeve order seems to have been the rule, again with the blue sash and dark-covered colonial helmet.

There are no commercial models which closely approximate these uniforms, and only the more experienced will wish to 'scratch-build' with nothing to start on. However, with the head from a British Zulu War figure and a torso, legs and arms selected from the Historex spares range, something might be achieved by the older and more expert modeller.

six

World War 1

At the outbreak of war the two regular regiments, the 1st and 2nd RE at Sidi-bel-Abbès and Saida respectively, each supported a 'march regiment' in Morocco. Most of the German and Austrian légionnaires were transferred to these units, though some chose to waive their traditional right as légionnaires not to have to fight against their own countrymen. A flood of 'duration only' volunteers swamped recruiting stations in France, and these were formed into two further *régiments de marche*, trained and stiffened by cadres of NCOs from Algeria and Morocco and by drafts of veterans. Designated '2nd Marching Regiment of the 1st Foreign Regiment' and '2nd Marching Regiment of the 2nd Foreign Regiment', these units will be referred to hereafter as the 2/1st and 2/2nd respectively. They were based at Avignon and Toulouse, and each comprised three 'raw' battalions and one veteran battalion. The two types of légionnaire did not mix happily at all, as was hardly surprising. The 'real' Legion types, veterans of Tonkin and Morocco, felt that the character of the corps was being let down by allowing all these soft odds and ends in, on the flimsy excuse of a World War!

Designated the Legion Brigade, the regiments were sent in October 1914 to a quiet sector of the front near Prunay as part of the Moroccan Division, staying there until April 1915. In December 1914 yet a third marching regiment affiliated to the 1st RE was formed; the 3/1st was largely made up of Russians, Italians and Belgians. Posted to Santerre, this unit of three battalions was weak both in numbers and reliable officers and NCOs. Both these Legion sectors saw scattered fighting, but nothing very significant. The first winter in the makeshift trenches was hard on all of them, veterans and tyros alike. In March 1915 the 3/1st was disbanded, its personnel being sent back to their own national armies.

In November 1914 a 4/1st Regiment had been formed largely of Italians (Italy was not yet in the war) led by a grandson of Garibaldi and including no less than five members of the famous revolutionary's family. Popularly known as the Garibaldi Brigade, the 4/1st saw action on Christmas Night 1914 at Bolante on the Argonne. An attack through woods was halted by the Germans, and the regiment lost 48 dead and 170 wounded. Two days later the Italians attacked once more, and managed to take and hold some enemy positions near Court-Chausses at a cost of 125 dead and 172 wounded — two Garibaldis were among the dead. The 4/1st was again heavily engaged in January 1915, but when Italy entered the war in May 1915 the survivors were transferred to the Italian Army. The 4/1st had lost 429 dead by then.

The 2/1st saw heavy fighting in May 1915 in the Artois battles; they advanced 3,000 yards in the face of withering fire, but were unable to hold on to the ground captured when the Germans counter-attacked, and in 24 hours lost 2,000 dead and wounded out of 4,000 men committed. The regiment was bloodied again near Berthonval Farm on June 15, without making significant headway. The 2/2nd had its first major engagement at Navarin Farm on September 27 1915. In two days' fighting the 1,600-strong unit was reduced to 800, gaining only a few yards. Several extraordinary feats of courage were recorded; and the buglers led the regiment over open ground swept by machine-gun fire, playing the Legion's famous march *Boudin*. In October 1915 the Moroccan Division was withdrawn from the line, by which time the colour of the 2/1st RE had been decorated with the *Croix de Guerre* and three palms. In view of heavy losses and dwindling recruiting, it was decided in November to fuse all Legion elements in France into a single unit — the *Régiment de Marche de la Légion Etrangère,* or RMLE for short. Still attached to the Moroccan Division, the RMLE, of three battalions initially and commanded by Colonel Cot, adopted the colour of the 2/1st RE.

On July 4 1916 the RMLE took part in an attack as part of the French Somme offensive, taking the village of Belloy-en-Santerre and holding it against German counter-attacks for a loss of 25 officers and 844 men. Briefly relieved, it was committed again on the night of July 7-8 at Chancelier, but was unable to make much progress despite 400 casualties.

The next major Legion battle was on April 17 1917 at Auberive, an attack on the German-held village of that name in the Suippes valley. A hideous struggle in deep mud lasted for five days and nights, but despite capturing two square kilometres largely with the grenade (some 50,000 were expended) the Legion was unable to secure the planned objectives and was pulled out after suffering ghastly casualties. The following month the RMLE passed under the command of Lieutenant-Colonel Rollet, 'The Father of the Legion'. This extraordinary officer, a veteran of the Moroccan mounted companies, was brave, hot-tempered, eccentric, and devoted to his temperamental regiment. Later a general, he became the first Inspector-General of the Legion, and served in that post until he died, greatly mourned, at Sidi-bel-Abbès in 1941. He was ordered to Paris with a colour-party in July 1917, and on Bastille Day the colour was decorated with the *Médaille Militaire* — partly in honour of its combat record, and partly to give tacit recognition to the fact that during the French Army mutinies of 1917 the RMLE had remained unshaken. The flag was now the most decorated of

any in the French Army.

The lanyard of the *Légion d'Honneur* would be added to the flag in September as a result of a successful engagement in August near Verdun-Cumieres. The RMLE took nearly two miles of ground for only 350 casualties — cheap, by contemporary standards.

In January 1918 the RMLE fought in Lorraine, and after a period of rest was put into the line again on April 24 to play a part in halting the German spring offensive. Their attack of the 26th at Hangard Wood against the German 19th Division was successful, but at fearful cost; one battalion was reduced to a single officer and 187 men, and one company was commanded by an experienced légionnaire in the absence of any higher rank. Total losses were around 850 officers and men.

Between May 24 and June 12 the RMLE fought around Soissons, and by the collapse of the enemy offensive on the latter date that phase of operations had cost the Legion 1,400 casualties. The RMLE was to the fore in French attacks of late July 1918, taking some eight miles of ground supported by tanks. The unit was kept in action for 13 days and nights during the attacks on the Hindenburg Line, and won a great deal of ground; by the time they were relieved most companies were down to about 50 men, often without a survivor above the rank of sergeant, and the battle as a whole reduced the RMLE to 700 men.

By the end of the war the flag of the RMLE was still the most decorated in the French Army. Of 42,883 men who had fought as légionnaires on the Western Front, 6,239 were Frenchmen and the rest foreigners from over a hundred countries. Some 115 officers and 5,172 men were killed in action, and 500 officers and more than 25,000 men were wounded or posted missing.

A battalion of the Legion served at Gallipoli with the *Régiment de Marche d'Algerie,* and later fought in Serbia. In 1919 a Legion battalion fought the Reds as part of the Allied expeditionary force in northern Russia.

French Foreign Legion

Corporal, Régiment de Marche de la Légion Etrangère, *1918. By the end of World War 1 the Legion was wearing absolutely regulation French infantry uniform and equipment, but in the khaki of the colonial troops rather than the horizon blue of the Line. This NCO wears a khaki-painted Adrian helmet, khaki greatcoat, khaki trousers and puttees. His leather equipment is black, his haversack fawn, and he carries the Lebel rifle. The collar insignia consists of a double green soutache and a green regimental number, on a khaki ground. The small wartime rank stripes are also green, worn on both cuffs; the three green service chevrons, indicating one full year of active service plus two further six-month periods, are worn on the left arm only. The RMLE's proud distinction was the double fourragère or lanyard, worn on the left shoulder in the colours of the medals awarded to the flag of the regiment: the green mixed with red of the* Croix de Guerre, *and the crimson of the* Légion d'Honneur, *each with a brass terminal* (Gerry Embleton).

Modelling the Legion: World War 1

The Legion wore the same uniforms as the rest of the French Army of the period, and is thus easy to model using any casting of *poilus* of 1914-18. At the beginning of the war the Legion wore their képis covered with a blue-grey sleeve; their blue-grey greatcoats bore the dark blue number of their regiment on the standing collar, and the uniform was completed by red trousers and black leather gaiters. In 1915 they went briefly into horizon blue, with yellow distinctives, but later that year changed into the khaki uniforms and steel helmets of all colonial troops, with green distinctives. The coat and tunic collars bore the numbers '1' or '2' within double green soutaches; senior NCOs and officers wore a gold grenade badge on the collar.

back to Africa, and a period of great expansion began in the Legion as the thousands of refugees left stranded and in some cases nationless by the Armistice flocked into the recruiting stations. In July 1920 the RMLE became the 3rd Foreign Regiment of Infantry — 3rd REI. Simultaneously the

Between the wars

The outbreak of World War 1, and the large drafts for the Western Front, left the Legion in Morocco with only five battalions and three mounted companies: the 1st, 2nd and 6th Battalions of the 1st RE, with two mounted companies, and the 3rd and 6th Battalions and one mounted company of the 2nd RE. Early in 1916 a mixed battalion of légionnaires and African Light Infantry was scraped together in Algeria and posted to the Bou Denib area. Lyautey, the famous governor-general of Morocco, was told in 1914 that his garrisons would be stripped for France's European army, and that he should retreat into the coastal enclaves. He refused; by very skilful diplomacy and a lot of quick footwork on the part of the few Legion units left, he managed to hold down the whole country during the war, while still sending off to France all the troops demanded.

It was touch and go, however, and there were some unpleasant incidents. Some posts had to be abandoned in the face of tribal rebellions; at Gaouz in July 1918 a retreating company covered by one of the mounted companies lost over 50 dead. No recruits came through, or not enough to make up losses, anyway — all the European countries were committed to a war which sucked up all they could offer in the way of fighting men. By 1920 the Legion in Morocco had only four battalions — the 6/2nd RE had been disbanded — with a total effective strength of only six companies. The three mounted companies were also very weak in numbers.

In November 1919 the RMLE came

2nd Lieutenant of the 1st RE in 1923, wearing a khaki tunic with lighter coloured breeches. Note the gold collar grenades within green soutaches, and the short, wartime pattern single gold bar of rank on the cuff. The képi is dark blue and red with gold piping, and the double fourragère *or lanyard in the colours of the* Croix de Guerre *and* Légion d'Honneur *indicates that he served in the wartime RMLE (Ron Harris).*

Regimental badge of the 1st REC, introduced in 1939. Basically silver, it has segments of green (left) red (right) and blue (bottom) enamel. (R. G. Windrow Collection).

four remaining battalions of the old 1st and 2nd RE in Morocco were fused into a strong new regiment, the 4th REI. The two mounted companies in the north of the country were now attached to the 3rd REI, and that based at Bou Denib to the 4th REI. A new 2nd REI was raised in December, of three battalions for Moroccan service, and moved from its old base at Saida in Algeria. In January 1921 the 1st REI was created at Sidi-bel-Abbès, retaining that station as the central depot of the Legion but providing battalions (it soon rose to a strength of six in all) for Morocco as needed. In 1921 another new regiment was created, largely from White Russian personnel with recent military experience — the 1st Foreign Cavalry (1st REC), at Saida. This was a mounted regiment, but in fact events in Morocco overtook it and the first elements were pressed into service as infantry at one stage.

In 1921-23 the 2nd, 3rd and 4th REI took part in numerous actions both large and small as they helped pacify the Tache de Taza, mountainous heart of Moroccan resistance. A line of blockhouses in the Oujda-Taza-Fez area — the Middle Atlas — was established, the battalions being split up into many tiny garrisons on arid ridges and peaks in a net to hold the tribesmen down.

In the Rif mountains to the north, in Spanish Morocco, the able nationalist leader Abd-el-Krim began his rebellion against the Spanish occupation troops. Educated, astute, well connected in Europe, and with a clear understanding of the importance of world opinion, Krim gathered a tribal army partly trained by Legion deserters, and even scraped together some artillery. His massacre of General Silvestre's army at Anual in July 1921 brought him the modern weapons and ammunition he needed — 12,000 dead men leave a lot of useful hardware lying on a battlefield — and he declared a Republic of the Rif, preparing to expel both Spanish and French from his country. In this he was ill-advised; had he concentrated on the Spanish colony and used his contacts to reassure the French, he might have succeeded. As it was he took on too many enemies at once. The Spanish and French were forced into each others' arms; but not before Krim had achieved considerable successes.

In April-May 1924 Krim's Beni-Uriaghel tribe crossed the frontier and attacked pro-French tribes such as the Beni-Zeroual; they did not enjoy much success, and the French pushed their blockhouse line another ten kilometres nearer the frontier, using garrisons of Turcos and Senegalese — it was considered to be country too favourable for desertions . for the Legion to be posted there. Lyautey expected the worst and asked for reinforcements; he was promised ten battalions, but only a few had arrived when, in April 1925, the storm broke.

With about 30,000 tribesmen, Krim made a determined push towards Fez, and by April 27 was within 30 kilometres of the capital. Nine French posts were captured, and 30 had to be hastily abandoned out of a total of 66. Without any real strategy, Krim was surprised by his success and halted a while in confusion, allowing frantic assembly of reinforcements. Companies and battalions were scraped together on an *ad hoc* basis throughout the line of Legion posts in the Taza corridor, and rushed to the threatened sectors. Local risings were put down after bloody fighting, allowing concentration on the point of greatest danger in the north. Elements of the 1st, 2nd, 3rd and 4th REI and the 1st REC saw much action during the counter-attacks of July and August 1925, particularly the 6th and 7th Battalions of the 1st REI. 50 battalions of fresh troops, mostly from the occupation army in the Rhineland, were rushed to Morocco, and in the spring of 1926 a massive combined Franco-Spanish advance into the Rif took place; eight Legion battalions took part. On May 26 Krim surrendered, and all conquered territory was recovered. In July the last dissidents in the Tache de Taza were rooted out by French forces including the whole 3rd REI,

and two battalions each of the 1st and 4th REI.

The penetration of the southern half of Morocco, and the establishment of order in the remoter parts of the country occupied several Legion units — notably the cavalry and the mounted companies, and the 4th REI — until the mid-1930s. The 1st REI remained in Algeria while the 2nd, 3rd and 4th remained in Morocco for the rest of the inter-war period. Altogether, between 1914-1935, Morocco cost the Legion 78 officers, 198 NCOs and 1,568 legionnaires dead, apart from many thousands of wounded.

Syria

Syria was granted to France as a mandate territory after World War 1, and in 1921 a battalion of the 4th REI was sent to occupy it, followed by another a few months later (these were the 4th and 5th Battalions). The 4th was sent home after three years of policing duties, and the 5th remained in garrison supported by the 4th Squadron of the 1st REC.

Trooper of the 1st REC, the regiment which nearly had its own 'Camerone' at Rachaya in Syria. For desert warfare the cavalry wore pale khaki gandouras — loose, simple coats based on native clothing — and covered képis with neckcloths of white or fawn. A Benigni painting (Képi Blanc).

In July 1925 the fanatical Druze tribesmen rose, and streamed down from the hills. The Legion moved into the hills to block their advance, and in September the 29th Company 4th REI and the cavalry squadron were surrounded and attacked at Messifre, a

A sergeant of Legion infantry in winter service dress of the 1930s. The tunic and half-breeches are khaki, and the puttees are made from old khaki coat-cloth. The képi, still rather low and crumpled in profile, has a midnight-blue band and a red top, black peak and chinstrap, and gold grenade badge and false chinstrap. Four lines of midnight-blue piping rise at front, back, and sides, ending in the circle of similar piping which runs round the edge of the slightly countersunk top surface. The neck-stock is light khaki; the blue sash is worn beneath the waist-belt which, like the three Lebel pouches and the bayonet frog, were worn in both black and brown leather depending upon local magazine stocks. The collar insignia of NCOs from this rank upwards was a gold grenade on a khaki patch edged with two green soutaches; other ranks wore green regimental numbers instead of the grenade. The two gold chevrons of rank are worn on both forearms; the single gold service stripe, denoting that this NCO is in his second five-year engagement, appears on the upper left arm only. In summer a pale sandy-drill uniform of similar cut was worn, often with the tunic skirts tucked inside the half-breeches and the sash concealing the join. Rank and service stripes and collar badges were fixed to the summer uniform with hook-and-eye or press-stud fastening, so that it could be washed conveniently. Soldats première classe wore single green chevrons, caporals two green chevrons. The service stripes followed the colour of the rank chevron — ie were in green for ranks below sergeant. Metal regimental, battalion and even company badges began to appear during the 1930s, and when worn were pinned to the right breast of the tunic (Gerry Embleton).

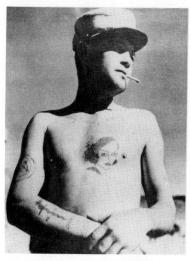

Crudely but comprehensively tattooed légionnaire of the 1930s. Tattoos have always been popular — one soldier caused endless trouble by having a very rude word tattooed across the palm of his right hand, thus silently expressing his opinion whenever he saluted an officer or senior NCO. He spent a lot of time on charges before it was decided to issue him with a glove . . . (Ron Harris).

Pensive legionnaire of the 4th REI, Morocco, 1939; note regimental badge (Ron Harris).

little mountain village, by some 3,000 warriors. For ten hours the légionnaires defended themselves against waves of attackers, often in hand-to-hand fighting; had not French aircraft appeared on the afternoon of the second day, and bombed and strafed the tribesmen until they withdrew, the situation might have become desperate. The Legion lost 47 dead and 83 wounded in this battle.

In November 1925 the 4th Squadron/1st REC, down to 100 men, was stationed in the little hill fort of Rachaya. The fort was attacked by several thousand Druzes on the 20th, and during that night the warriors broke the perimeter and got inside the fort. Fighting went on inside the walls for three days, and the last enemy were only cleared by a desperate bayonet charge. Carrier pigeons were

sent off with appeals for help; the squadron suffered 40 per cent casualties and the survivors, reeling after three days and nights without sleep, were down to their last 15 rounds per man, and had used up their grenades. The commander, Captain Landriau, decided that if help did not arrive by the fourth night the survivors would 'faire Camerone' — fix bayonets and go out into the middle of the enemy in a last wild charge. The relief column arrived with hours to spare.

Scattered fighting went on until 1927 but there were no further really major battles. The Legion garrison was eventually raised to a strength of four battalions and a mounted company, and designated RLPO — 'Regiment of the Legion in the Near East'. In October 1939 this was redesignated 6th REI — the number '5' had gone to the Indo-China garrison battalions, formed into a single regiment in 1930.

At the outbreak of World War 2 the Legion thus consisted of the 1st REI (Algeria), 2nd, 3rd and 4th REI (Morocco), 5th REI (Indo-China), 6th REI (Syria), 1st REC (Tunisia) and the 2nd REC, formed in 1939 (Morocco).

French Foreign Legion

Modelling the Legion: 1919-39

Stadden make a 54 mm casting of a légionnaire in parade dress of 1939 vintage. Stadden French officers of World War 1, if given képis instead of helmets, could be finished as officers of 1920. Younger and less demanding modellers could make a reasonable facsimile of a légionnaire of the inter-war period by slightly modifying an Airfix 1:32 scale Japanese soldier, as in the illustration accompanying this chapter.

From 1927 onwards, though with a

Kit issue, 1939 — this picture, though not of high quality, shows the new cylindrical képi, the tunic and the half-breeches quite clearly (Ron Harris).

slight hangover of older uniforms due to administrative delays, the Legion wore a summer and a winter uniform of identical cut but different weights. The summer style was of light sand-coloured drill, the winter of khaki serge. Both consisted of a tunic with a falling collar of wide outline, no breast pockets, skirt pockets with an external, straight flap, and a single row of six buttons. Collar badges consisted of the regimental number enclosed by a double soutache, both in green. Rank chevrons in green were worn above both cuffs, point uppermost, and reaching from front to back seam of the sleeve; long service chevrons of the same design were worn (never more than three) on the left upper arm only. Sergeants and above wore gold

Stages in simple conversion of Airfix 1:32 scale Japanese infantry to Legion infantry of the 1920s and '30s.

Badge of the 4th REI, introduced 1937 — silver, red over green side stripes (R. G. Windrow Collection).

chevrons in both these positions. For parades the green epaulettes with red crescents and fringes were worn. The trousers were the same colour as the tunics, of pantaloon or semi-breeches cut, worn with puttees. The blue sash was worn at the waist under the leather belt and pouches, the tunic often being tucked into the trousers.

The World War 1 Lebel rifle and equipment were used until the late 1930s, and after then by some units. The képi retained its white or pale fawn cover when working or in the field, but neck-cloths do not seem to have been common. In 1939 a new képi appeared; for wear on all occasions rather than just on parade, it had a white cotton cover and was of stiff cylindrical outline. Sergeants removed their covers and at all times wore the dark blue képi with its red top and gold grenade badge exposed.

The cavalry regiments wore the same uniform but with silver instead of gold buttons, badges and chevrons, and black leather knee-gaiters instead of puttees. At various times during the 1930s the enamelled breast-badges appeared, worn on the right breast.

French Foreign Legion

eight

World War 2

In the years immediately before World War 2 the Nazis made use of the traditionally high recruitment of légionnaires among Germans to infiltrate agents into the Legion. The authorities recognised this, and hundreds of suspects were interned immediately war broke out. There was a natural reluctance to employ the Legion in Europe, however. Some 6,000 'duration only' volunteers were enrolled, most being posted to three 'marching regiments' in France for training. The 21st and 22nd RMVE — 'Marching Regiments of Foreign Volunteers' — appeared in October 1939 and the 23rd RMVE in May 1940. The quality of these units was not high; standards of discipline, equipment and leadership were poor, and they bore no real relation to the Legion proper.

After due consideration two further units were raised in the winter of 1939-40, consisting of French volunteers and drafts of reliable Africa veterans and designated 11th and 12th REI. Another unit formed for French service, with drafts from the two cavalry regiments, was a light armoured recce battalion designated GERD 97, attached to the 7th North African Division. Lastly, but most famous of all, the 13th *Demi-Brigade de la Légion Etrangère* — 13th DBLE — was formed early in 1940 for a planned Allied intervention in Finland. Since Finland fell before it could be deployed it completed its Arctic training in France, and was sent to Narvik as part of the Allied landing force in Norway in May 1940.

One and a half companies had been lost by the time this battalion was shipped out, after distinguishing itself in battle against the Germans. It returned to Brest, and went into action against the invaders near Rennes. When the cease-fire was announced Colonel Monclar gave his men the choice of remaining in France or following de Gaulle to England; most opted to continue the fight.

Légionnaires of the 13th DBLE in the Libyan desert, 1942; note British tropical uniforms with addition of French M1936 rifles and old leather belt, Y-straps and cartridge pouches. The képis show signs of wear — they could not be replaced between 1940 and 1943, when the Allied advance into Vichy-held North Africa released stocks (Imperial War Museum).

Meanwhile the other Legion units in France had been heavily engaged. Between May 27 and June 11 the 11th REI put up a stubborn defence at Inor Wood between the Meuse and the Chiers before, reduced to half strength, they disappeared into the chaos of retreat, after burning their colours. The 12th REI was reduced to third strength in 36 hours' fierce fignt-ing near Soissons on June 6, and was for all intents and purposes destroyed. The 21st RMVE broke under heavy attack in the Ardennes on June 10, and the 22nd RMVE did rather better at Peronne before being reduced to half strength and smashed in a three-day battle with German armour. The 23rd RMVE, poorly equipped and unready, still held up enemy tanks for two days near Soissons before being forced to withdraw on June 17. GERD 97 made contact on the Somme on May 18 and fought courageously for the next three weeks in a series of delaying actions aginst superior forces. On June 9 the unit made a furious counter-attack on German armour and was virtually annihilated.

The Armistice and the rise of Vichy put the Legion in an evil position. For the time being the regiments in Algeria, Morocco, Tunisia and Syria were left to carry on their garrison duties, but they were harassed by inspections and enquiries from Ger-man bureaux anxious to check on personnel. These were usually circumvented by sending men likely to

The Free French forces in Africa devised armoured vehicles — armoured patrol trucks and portees for 75 mm guns — by plating Chev-rolet trucks and fitting automatic weapons. Here, the leader of a patrol checks their position (Imperial War Museum).

attract the attention of the Boches off into the desert on long training exer-cises when the inspections were imminent. Légionnaires liable to attract German interest were also shipped to Indo-China; and the 4th REI, newly designated 4th DBLE, was quietly filled out with such fugitives

The Free French General Catroux decorates a Legion major with the Offi-cer's Cross of the Légion d'Honneur at a parade in Damascus after the fall of Vichy Syria to the Allies (Imper-ial War Museum).

Legion Bren carrier on patrol near Bir Hakeim, 1942 — note FM24/29 fitted on anti-aircraft mounting. The commander has a diamond in vertical stripes of blue, white and red painted on the left side of his British helmet (Imperial War Museum).

and transferred to Senegal, where even the most officious Nazi was unlikely to follow. Recruiting was naturally very slow, and the 2nd REI was disbanded. The reduced 1st stayed in Algeria and the 3rd in Morocco; the 1st REC took in the useful men from the 2nd REC, which was also disbanded. Despite the cat-and-mouse games with the Nazis some 2,000 men were combed out by the Germans, their countrymen, and formed into a Wehrmacht regiment for desert service — the 361st Infantry Regiment which served with honour in the Afrika Korps' 90th Light Division.

The 13th DBLE in England was brought to a strength of two battalions and in December 1940 was used in the French Cameroons. It was shipped to Port Sudan in February 1941, and fought alongside British troops at Keren and, particularly, Massawa. On June 8 1941 a joint force of British and Free French passed from Jordan into Vichy Syria, and the 13th DBLE was with the Damascus column. A tragic echo of Barbastro was heard at Damas in the Syrian hills, when légionnaires of the 6th REI and the 13th DBLE met in battle. The fighting was very fierce, and casualties were heavy, but both sides treated each other as comrades when it came to taking prisoners or picking up wounded. The 13th DBLE won the day, and when Syria was turned over to the Free French the 6th REI was disbanded. Some 1,000 of the men accepted an offer to join the 13th DBLE as a third battalion, but only two officers. An able and popular officer, the Georgian Prince Colonel Amilakvari, took over the 13th DBLE in August 1941.

In February 1942 the 13th DBLE was posted to Bir Hakeim, a defensive position at the very southern tip of British 8th Army's lines in the Western Desert. On May 27 Italian armour attacked fiercely, and by nightfall 32 tanks lying silent under the desert moon testified to the skill of the Legion. On June 2 a major attack by the Afrika Korps, supported by Stukas, opened; and for nine days the Legion and the other Free French units held out against incessant pressure from all sides. Receiving orders to withdraw, they slipped through the minefields without mishap on the night of June 10.

Splendidly bearded Legion NCO with company mascot — note Lebel 8 mm carbine of 1916 vintage slung on his back (Imperial War Museum).

The Legion was heavily committed to attacks at El Himeimat, on the extreme left flank of the Alamein line, on October 23 1942, and on that day Colonel Amilakvari, a Legion veteran since 1924, was killed at the head of his men. The 13th DBLE remained with 8th Army all the way to Tunisia. When the Anglo-American forces landed at Oran on November 8 1942 the 1st REI was ordered to resist, but deliberately dragged its feet until Vichy forces capitulated. When the final battles against the Tunisian bridgehead began the North African regiments of the Legion (including the hastily returned 4th DBLE) raised two *régiments de marche* to fight with the Allies — the 1st and 3rd REIM. The cavalry mustered a small mechanised combat group. This latter captured a German position at Foum el Gouafel on January 11 1943, without suffering any deaths. The 3rd REIM, eager for battle, got into difficulties on the Jebel Mansour during the Kasserine battles;

the 1st REIM was also committed alongside British 1st Army. In February the 13th DBLE, advancing with 8th Army from Libya, was badly cut up in a two-day battle at Jebel Garci. Eventually the 1st REIM, now issued with modern Allied hardware, fought at Pont du Fahs and Zaghouan in May, with notable spirit and success. The German 361st Regiment was interned after the Axis surrender in Africa, but many were allowed to rejoin the Legion in 1945.

By this time Legion strength in North Africa was well below 10,000 men, and some reorganisation was obviously necessary. The best men, equipped and uniformed by the American army, were formed into the second RMLE to appear in 30 years. With the 1st REC providing light armoured support, this armoured infantry regiment rode its half-tracks into Europe as part of the 5th Moroccan Division. Landing in southern France in September 1944, the Legion

A young captain of the 13th DBLE in the Western Desert; note three rank bars on slip-on shoulder strap tally, unit number in 'bomb' of gold grenade badge, and three rank stripes in gold around upper part of képi (Imperial War Museum).

Légionnaires of the 13th DBLE in a sangar — a dry-stone defence emplacement; note battered képis and British battledress (Imperial War Museum).

distinguished itself in the final campaign through Alsace-Lorraine into Germany. The RMLE won a notable victory at Belfort in November 1944, and again at Colmar in February 1945. The légionnaires forged on eastwards through Stuttgart and Friedrichshafen, and the dawn of VE Day found them at Arlberg in Austria.

The 13th DBLE remained independent, fighting with the 5th Army in Italy in 1944 until moved to France in August. It fought near Toulon and Lyons, and was with the RMLE at Colmar.

Meanwhile, in Indo-China, the 5th REI had had a very different sort of war, and in many ways a worse one. Vichy had allowed the Japanese to occupy the country without a fight, in return for which the French colonial administration was kept in being, though in a frustrating and humiliating atmosphere. In March 1945 the Japanese ordered the disarmament and internment of the remaining French troops under arms; some units resisted, and were treated with the utmost brutality by the Japanese. The 3,000 légionnaires, incensed by this, determined to fight their way into Allied China. During an epic 500 mile jungle march which lasted 52 days, the 5th REI beat off numerous attacks and

Fine study of 13th DBLE légionnaire in British battledress with improvised green grenade collar badges on khaki patches, and M1936 rifle (Imperial War Museum).

burst through many Japanese ambushes before crossing the frontier into Yunnan. They remained in China until French troops landed at Hanoi in April 1946, and then marched back again. So many of them were time-expired that the regiment was soon disbanded, however.

Modelling the Legion: 1939-45

The 13th DBLE was uniformed by British Army stores before it joined 8th Army, and wore normal British khaki drill shorts and shirts and serge battledress until 1943. The accompanying photos show that French leather equipment was still worn, and M1936 rifles and FM24/29 light machine-guns were used. The képis tended to be very battered, as no replacements were available. Green cut-out grenade badges were sewn on the collars of the battledress. NCO ranks were indicated by small reversed chevrons in green or gold, either on the upper arm or slipped on to the shoulder-strap on a cloth loop. Officers wore the usual French rank bars around their shoulder-straps.

The regimental badge of the Legion's 13th Half-Brigade, instituted in 1946 and still in use: a blue Cross of Lorraine on a white field supported by green over red bars, with a gold grenade, dragon, scroll, and trim (R. G. Windrow Collection).

When the RMLE was equipped with US Army clothing in 1943, only the rank insignia, and in certain cases the headgear, distinguished them from American troops. Képis were worn when not in action; and officers and senior NCOs wore dark green side-caps with red tops. (The cavalrymen of the REC wore dark green with dark blue tops.)

The REC wore US single-piece tank suits, and a mixture of American and French tank crew helmets. They drove Greyhound armoured cars, and the RMLE rode in White M-3 half-tracks.

Modelling all these troops is a simple matter, from any of the many metal and Airfix plastic figures of US and British soldiers of the 1939-45 period. The Tamiya plastic kit figures of British and US infantry are probably the most suitable in 1:35 scale, while in 1:32 the Airfix 8th Army Multipose pack will be useful.

Those units which were in Vichy territory until a later stage of the war continued to wear pre-war Legion uniform.

nine

Indo-China 1946-1954

There was a fatal hiatus of power in Indo-China at the end of World War 2. Immediately after the Japanese surrender the Vietnamese guerrillas who had fought the occupiers, armed with weapons supplied by the Allies and now with those taken from the disarmed Japanese troops, announced by word and deed their determination that the French would not be allowed to step back into the role of colonial masters as if nothing had happened. In this situation of political complexity the hasty transfer of a small British force did little good apart from providing a semblance of law and order. It was early 1946 before the French returned in strength. Ho Chi Minh, leader of the nationalists and Communists, negotiated with them briefly, but his demands and the concessions France's disorganised post-war government were willing to make were too far apart; and shortly afterwards he took his Viet-Minh guerrillas back into the countryside and began a war of attrition which quickly escalated into the largest and worst of the post-colonial conflicts which troubled the world in the aftermath of global war.

Virtually the whole fighting strength of a Foreign Legion vastly swollen by the tens of thousands of post-war refugees and displaced persons characteristic of Europe in 1945-55 was soon committed to this dirty, heartbreaking war. First to arrive was a hastily formed RMEO — 'Far East Marching Regiment' — formed from the first combat-ready elements of depot troops and new recruits in North Africa in 1945, and shipped out to South Annam in February 1946. This unit was redesignated 2nd REI shortly afterwards; it saw constant hard fighting from the first, and lost 300 dead in its first few months of operations.

In March 1946 the 13th DBLE arrived, and its separated battalions fought for two years in Cochin China in the extreme south. By June the new 3rd REI, formed from the wartime RMLE, had arrived; after heavy fighting in Annam it was shifted north to Tonkin. The 4th REI was re-created in 1946 but remained in Morocco, as the 1st REI remained in Algeria. They became depot regiments, training and sending out East regular drafts of recruits for the fighting regiments, and receiving returned veterans from that theatre.

The 6th REI was briefly re-formed in 1947 in Tunisia, but served mainly as a pool of manpower for Indo-China and was dissolved again, and finally, in 1951. Drafts from this and the 4th Regiment formed the re-born 5th REI

Badge of the 1e RE, the depot and administrative regiment of the Legion; it was worn by the Groupement Autonome de la Légion Etrangère until 1955, when the 1st Regiment took over these functions. In white, it bears the design of the campaign medal ribbon awarded for the Mexican campaign of 1862-67: a red (top left to bottom right) and green saltire, a black eagle, and a green snake, all trimmed in gold.

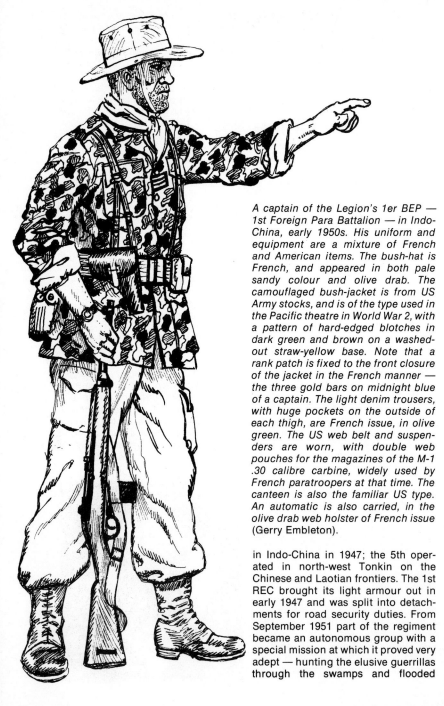

A captain of the Legion's 1er BEP — 1st Foreign Para Battalion — in Indo-China, early 1950s. His uniform and equipment are a mixture of French and American items. The bush-hat is French, and appeared in both pale sandy colour and olive drab. The camouflaged bush-jacket is from US Army stocks, and is of the type used in the Pacific theatre in World War 2, with a pattern of hard-edged blotches in dark green and brown on a washed-out straw-yellow base. Note that a rank patch is fixed to the front closure of the jacket in the French manner — the three gold bars on midnight blue of a captain. The light denim trousers, with huge pockets on the outside of each thigh, are French issue, in olive green. The US web belt and suspenders are worn, with double web pouches for the magazines of the M-1 .30 calibre carbine, widely used by French paratroopers at that time. The canteen is also the familiar US type. An automatic is also carried, in the olive drab web holster of French issue (Gerry Embleton).

in Indo-China in 1947; the 5th operated in north-west Tonkin on the Chinese and Laotian frontiers. The 1st REC brought its light armour out in early 1947 and was split into detachments for road security duties. From September 1951 part of the regiment became an autonomous group with a special mission at which it proved very adept — hunting the elusive guerrillas through the swamps and flooded

French Foreign Legion

Legion paratroopers of the élite 1st BEP in Indo-China, 1953, wearing camouflage jackets, olive green trousers and green berets; they carry the M1949 sub-machine-gun (E.C.P. Armees).

paddy fields in amphibious armoured vehicles provided by the Americans, the so-called 'Crabs' and 'Alligators'. The 2nd REC was also re-formed but remained in Morocco.

In 1948 the Legion's élite 1st Parachute Battalion — 1st BEP — was formed, and in late 1948 it arrived in Indo-China where it was used as a mobile striking force. In January 1949 the 2nd BEP also arrived, and after operations in the south moved up to the Tonkin Delta in 1950. Like the 1st BEP, it was to see numerous battles all over Indo-China in the next few years, being shifted at need from one end of the country to the other.

There is no space here, and little point, in attempting a history of the war, however brief. Its general pattern has become all too familiar, and it has to be said that though the French troops fought with great tenacity and courage their generals were unequal to this new type of campaign. The guerrillas, invisible among the mass of the population, came out at night to mine roads, attack isolated posts, and infiltrate the peaceful population. Their spies were everywhere, and despite resorting to harsh methods of

intelligence-gathering, the French were always two jumps behind the elusive Viet-Minh. The available troops had to be split up into hundreds of small company-size garrisons whose influence rarely extended beyond rifle-range in daytime, or beyond the edge of the light shed by their arc-lights at night.

After dark the Viets took over the whole country except the garrison towns; and as they grew stronger and more confident, the remoter areas became unsafe for all but strong convoys in daytime. Ambushes and raids were constant. Mobile striking groups, of which the best were made up of légionnaires and French paratroopers, tried to anticipate the Viet manoeuvres or at least to pursue them to destruction afterwards; but despite considerable local success the overall picture was discouraging. The flower of France's post-war army fell in bloody, pointless skirmishes, and the people at home were weary of war and grief. Successive governments of unprecedented instability and lack of integrity consistently let the fighting army down by their ill-conceived political manoeuvres, and in Indo-China all the efforts of the better officers were hamstrung by corruption among the local administrators and native authorities.

A few Legion battles may be mentioned briefly, as representative of a campaign which cost the Legion 314 officers, 1,071 NCOs and no less than 8,997 men dead in battle or died of wounds.

The small, isolated Legion posts which guarded the road and river highways of the country were always vulnerable. In bad terrain such as heavily jungled mountains the relief columns summoned by radio could only approach along single roads, easily blocked by the Viets; often the columns were ambushed and wiped out in their turn, and if they did get through to the besieged forts it was often too late to do anything but bury the dead and wearily rebuild the defences before leaving another lonely company isolated in the mountain mists. Occasionally, however, the légionnaires — among them hardened veterans of half a dozen World War 2 armies — managed to hold out and convince the Viets that the time was not yet ripe for all-out attack.

At the fort of Phu Tong Hoa in July 1948 was a single company of the 3rd REI numbering 104 men. They were attacked at night by three battalion-sized units of the Viet-Minh with massive mortar support. They held out and repulsed the attack at a cost of 55 casualties, and when the relief force arrived next day they were greeted by an honour guard of survivors in dress uniforms, turned out in parade-ground perfection by the senior surviving NCO.

In September 1950 the Viet-Minh General Giap, having progressed with the training and equipment of his Communist-supplied regulars, began his campaign to drive the French from Tonkin. The line of forts on the ridges which command the valleys of the Red and Black Rivers of the Delta were an obvious first step.

Dong Khe was a little post which had already seen much fighting. In May 1950 the garrison, two companies of North African *tirailleurs,* had been wiped out. Paratroopers re-took the fort and after a sweep in the area by two battalions calm seemed to have been restored. The next garrison was from the 8th *Tabor* of Moroccan infantry, and in September 1950 the 5th and 6th Companies of the 3rd REI took over.

The fort was a typical construction of its type — earth banks and trenches with sharpened bamboo and barbed wire defences surrounding sand-bagged dug-outs and bastions and a group of permanent buildings, placed on a hill-top with the jungle cleared back on the crown to give a field of fire. It had two artillery pieces, a 57 mm and a 105 mm howitzer. A second Dong Khe also existed nearby: the full-scale model constructed by the 174th Regiment of the Viet-Minh army, for its careful and lengthy training exercises.

On September 16 six battalions of Viets attacked the two French com-

Early French camouflage smock worn by paratrooper of the early 1950s — a pull-over type with a built-in hood (J. P. Benavente).

Later French camouflage uniform and steel helmet, worn with mixture of US and French webbing (J. P. Benavente).

French Foreign Legion

panies under cover of a heavy artillery and mortar barrage; four of the five perimeter outposts were wiped out, and all day the Viets fought to get a lodgement on the main position. During the night they succeeded in capturing many of the bastions, which then began to change hands as furious counter-attacks alternated between Legion and Viet positions. The fighting was at a range of a few yards, and often closed to hand-to-hand. The garrison managed to repair the radio next day, for long enough to receive a message from Hanoi promising that the Ist BEP, dropped nearby, would come to their aid that night. But the paratroopers ran into fierce resistance — Giap had deployed other troops in a security cordon round his battle — and never managed to reach the fort. The following night Dong Khe fell. The two companies lost 85 dead, and 140 wounded and captured, of whom not many survived in Viet hands. A handful of survivors of the last attack managed to creep away into the jungle and bring word to the nearest French positions.

Dong Khe was not an isolated incident but the signal for a major offensive. The paratroopers dropped near That Khe on September 17 in an attempt to fight their way through to Dong Khe were, on the 30th, attached to one of two four-battalion columns which attempted to clear the area of Viets. They never had a chance — surrounded in thick country by 30 Viet battalions, they were fighting for their lives within days, and found that even when they linked up they were blocked in every direction. Each little town they managed to fight their way into at the cost of more casualties had to be evacuated in its turn, the garrisons joining the mobile column. In heroic rearguard actions the 1st BEP was literally destroyed, losing all its officers except one, and 90 per cent of its men. The 3rd Battalion/3rd REI was also wiped out on this march, and the 2nd Battalion/3rd REI was very badly mauled.

The most famous battle of the war was, of course, the siege of Dien Bien Phu. The reasons why the French command decided to plant this entrenched camp and airstrip in the bottom of a bowl of hills, far behind enemy lines, are still being argued. The strategy is confused, and whatever it was it was based on a fatal underestimate of the progress made by Giap in training and equipping his divisions for conventional warfare. It was intended that the camp, held by 12 battalions of légionnaires, paras, North Africans and local troops, would be quite invulnerable to enemy attack. Its position would block all Viet moves on the Laotian border, and from its safe base paratroopers and tanks would strike outwards into the hills, extending its influence and control over a wide area. It would be supplied by air and its isolation 200 kilometres from Hanoi was thus unimportant. In November 1953 it was seized by an air-drop of six para battalions, and building began.

The camp consisted of a central position, with airstrip and dispersals for Bearcat fighters, emplacements for 28 heavy guns, and 12 Chaffee tanks, guarded by outlying and self-sufficient strongpoints arranged for all-round defence and placed as far as possible to cover one another. The lie of the land did not allow this at all points of the perimeter, however. At '12 o'clock' and '2 o'clock' from the centre were strongpoints *Gabrielle* and *Beatrice,* the latter held by the 3rd Battalion/13th DBLE. Closer in at '3 o'clock' was *Dominique,* then *Eliane* at '5 o'clock'; then far away, five kilometres due south, was *Isabelle* at '6 o'clock' with the 3rd Battalion/3rd REI. At '7 o'clock' in the main perimeter was *Claudine,* with the 1st Battalion/13th DBLE, then *Francoise* at '8 o'clock', then *Huguette* at '9 o'clock' with the 1st Battalion/2nd REI. *Anne-Marie* at '10 o'clock' completed the perimeter; and the 1st (and later, the 2nd) BEP formed part of the mobile reserve in the centre. The mortar companies of the 3rd and 5th REI, and a company of para-mortars, supplemented the artillery of Colonel Piroth — the artillery he was so confi-

Top left *The Legion's white képi (here, unfortunately, missing its black chin-strap) is worn with a pale khaki shirt, green tie, and battledress of similar colour to British issue. The epaulettes of parade uniform have straps of a rich blue-green and red crescents and fringes.* **Above right** *The dark blue sash is worn round the waist under the belt, here a US webbing type worn in the mid-1950s, whitened for parade wear.* **Top right** *On the left arm the corporal's stripes are repeated, and below them the badge of the Legion's rankers — a blue/black diamond with triple green edging and a green seven-flamed grenade. NCOs from sergeant up wear a gold grenade. The lanyard of the Croix de Guerre TOE — for overseas service — is worn by all ranks of the regiment; here it is in parade position. It is of pale blue cord with red flecks. The medal itself, in bronze, with a red-pale blue-red ribbon, is worn on the breast, indicating that the soldier has personally won this decoration.* **Above left** *A corporal's stripes, in green on black, are worn on the right arm. Many Legion soldiers have passed the para course, and the silver brevet with gold foliage sprays is pinned on the right breast. The badge of the 2nd REI since 1955 is silver, with vertical side bars of green (left) and red (right) on both sides. It bears a grenade and a horseshoe, in memory of the old Legion Mounted Companies, and is worn on a hanging fob from the pocket.*

Dummy dressed in the 1949 Legion battledress, now used only for parades; this uniform is correct for the period 1956-57.

carried in sections on the backs of 75,000 coolies up the jungle trails and installed in well-camouflaged positions; (c) the attackers and their guns would be defended by massive anti-aircraft artillery zones installed in the same way; and (d) that the battle would not be one of movement around a secure base, but a siege.

On March 13 1954 a tremendous artillery barrage opened, quickly exposing the inadequacy of the trenches, dug-outs and sandbag bastions to withstand heavy 105 mm shells. Piroth's guns proved hopelessly unable to silence the enemy batteries, and he committed suicide next day. Within two days *Beatrice* had been overrun and the 3rd Battalion/13th DBLE destroyed — 326 dead, missing or seriously wounded. *Gabrielle,* isolated, was abandoned. A few days later *Anne-Marie* was abandoned. The North African units were displaying poor morale, and in attempts to recapture some abandoned bastions the para reserves lost heavily. Many aircraft were destroyed, the remainder left for safety, and the garrison was penned in the perimeter; soon the airstrip was unusable and all supplies had to be air-dropped. French air force strikes on the artillery positions in the hills were unsuccessful, and tactical and supply aircraft began to fall in great numbers to the Communist anti-aircraft batteries. The 2nd BEP and untrained volunteers from the 3rd and 5th REI jumped into the camp at night early in April. Artillery fire and massive infantry attacks slowly chipped away the bastions, and in furious counter-attacks the paratroopers and tanks were whittled down until their strength was inadequate to achieve any lasting success at any point. The courage of the men and their officers was extraordinary, and their suffering appalling. Air-drops soon proved inadequate; food, ammunition and medical supplies all ran critically low, adding to the miseries of the garrison in a camp now feet deep in mud from the spring rains.

The final assault came on May 6, and by daybreak on the 7th only a

dent could silence all opposition, and which he did not bother to dig in any more thoroughly than would protect his crews from mortar fire . . . The rest of the garrison of 14,000 men consisted of French and Vietnamese paratroopers, Algerian and Moroccan *tirailleurs,* and Thai troops.

What the high command did not realise was that (a) Giap would accept the challenge with four divisions, regular troops trained and equipped by the Chinese; (b) they would be supported by some 200 artillery pieces, small area in the centre of the camp and the isolated *Isabelle* were still in French hands. By the early hours of the 8th the camp had fallen. At *Isabelle* the 3rd Battalion/3rd REI tried to break out; less than 100 reached French lines. Dien Bien Phu cost the Legion 1,500 dead and 4,000 wounded; it cost France Indo-China.

Modelling the Legion: Indo-China

The French Army in the immediate aftermath of World War 2 had to depend largely on American combat clothing. The Legion in Indo-China wore olive drab combat uniforms of US type in the early stages, usually with bush-hats. In the last half of the war French olive green drill clothing was issued, characterised by large pockets on the outside of the thighs. The bush-hat remained the usual headgear except when in close fighting, but as time went on and artillery became a feature of the war the US steel helmet was worn, sometimes with netting covers. US webbing equipment and small arms were the norm, although the M1949 sub-machine-gun was issued in great numbers, particularly to the paratroopers. These latter wore US printed camouflage suits of the type used in the Pacific campaigns of World War 2; sometimes the jackets of this suit were worn with olive green trousers. The paras wore bush-hats or green berets when not in action. The French camouflage pattern clothing familiar from the Algerian War reached some paratroop units late in the campaign. The képi was worn when not in the front line, white-covered or uncovered depending on rank. Pale khaki drill shirts, slacks and shorts were worn in summer as service dress, with the addition of Legion epaulettes, sashes, and whitened belts and gaiters for parade purposes.

Modellers are largely on their own resources for reproducing this period; basic castings and Airfix plastic figures of US or Australian troops can be converted without much trouble, and képis added from scrap. Typical small arms of the war available to modellers are the Thompson sub-machine-gun, the M1 Garand rifle and the M1 .30 cal carbine with solid or skeleton stock.

ten

The last twenty years

The Algerian War in which the Legion last saw heavy fighting does not lend itself to detailed description in a book of this sort; unlike Indo-China, it did not consist of even a few pitched battles. The pattern was one of constant dreary patrolling, occasional sweeps against the ALN in the mountainous areas, and urban security. One or two general points need to be made, perhaps.

Firstly, the French were winning the war militarily when they lost it politically — uniquely in modern history, they had forced the ALN to revert from one phase of Mao's prescribed sequence of guerrilla warfare to an earlier phase by determined and intelligent offensives. Secondly, the bulk of the huge French forces in Algeria were made up of conscripts who were unsympathetic to the aims of the war, and who could only be relied upon to carry out routine security duties, while the main burden of aggressive warfare fell on the Legion and the parachute regiments. Thirdly, the bad name which certain French units were given in the world Press for brutality to prisoners and ill-treatment during interrogation needs to be examined rather carefully before one accepts it at face value.

The ALN used methods of even greater ruthlessness in their campaign to swing a largely apathetic civilian population behind their cause; and as the British have discovered in Ulster and the Americans in Vietnam, the only way to fight fire is with fire. If one is opposed by a ruthless urban or rural guerrilla enemy, who uses physical terror as a major weapon in his arsenal both to cow civilians and to tempt the occupying forces into retaliating in kind, then one has a simple choice: renounce the methods of the enemy, and lose, in the certainty that the world Press will declare you used them anyway; or use them, and win, and be damned to world opinion. It is not a choice anyone who has not faced it should regard lightly, from the comfort of their armchair.

The whole Legion was committed to the war in Algeria. The 1st RE (now a depot unit pure and simple, without a combat role) nevertheless mounted small combat operations in the immediate vicinity of Sidi-bel-Abbès, supporting among other *ad hoc* units a light armoured patrol company. The 2nd REI patrolled Southern Oran province from Ain Sefra to Géryville as a motorised infantry battalion. (The regiments were reduced to single battalion size from 1957 on; the number of companies varied and depended on how many support and specialist companies were attached at any one time.) The 3rd REI had responsibility for the mountains of Kabylia, always one of the hot spots of Algerian fighting. The 4th REI came back to Algeria from Morocco in 1958 and operated in south-east Algeria from Tebessa, guarding the Tunisian frontier. The 5th REI was based around Tlemcen and Arzew, and the 13th DBLE fought in the Aures Mountains. Both cavalry regiments patrolled the Tunisian Barrage and the Moroccan border, and were split up to provide armoured car support for various drives in other parts of the country. The 1st REP — descendants of the martyred 1st BEP, formed again in 1955 — were based at Zeralda after taking part in the Suez campaign of 1956. Like the 2nd REP, at Philippeville, they formed part of the French mobile striking force, and took part in many stiff engagements; the 1st REP was one of the units of General Massu's division which crushed ALN terrorism in Algiers itself in a matter of weeks. The colourful desert patrol companies, the CSPLs which had been raised progressively in 1940, 1946, 1949 and 1956, continued their traditional role of patrolling the oases on the fringes of the great sand sea.

The Generals' Revolt of 1961, an unhappy episode in French history, may be briefly described as the backlash of an army which felt itself betrayed by its political masters. The army had been wary of French governments ever since Indo-China; why not, since the army had paid so grievously for political mistakes there? In Algeria, where they knew they were winning a war to keep the country French and where there was a substantial European population with whom many officers and men had ties, they were suddenly informed that the new de Gaulle government intended to give away what they had bled so freely to defend. British armies have been faced with the same situation several times in the past decades, and although the centuries-old tradition of a completely non-political army has saved us from such episodes as Algiers 1961, it has sometimes caused very depressed morale. After the agony of Indo-China, this final betrayal — as they saw it — was too much for some French units, notably the 1st REP. They carried out an almost bloodless coup in Algiers and called on other units to support them. The call was not heeded. The regiment was disbanded, and the officers of this and other Legion regiments were ruthlessly purged, many being imprisoned. As a whole, the Legion remained loyal to the legal government, however.

It was some time before the authorities felt they could trust the Legion again, and there was a period of uncalled-for and petty slights to the corps' honour. All is forgiven (if not forgotten) now, however, and the Legion is back in its rightful place as one of France's élite combat units. After an emotional departure from Sidi-bel-Abbès, Saida, and all the other homes they had known for generations in a country they had done so much to create, the Legion installed itself — smaller, but still potent — in new quarters.

The 1st RE and the central facilities are at Aubagne, near Marseilles. Not far away the 1st REC has its armoured

a

b

a *Infantry and cavalry wear this badge in gold and silver respectively on the green beret issued as working dress since 1956. Paras wear the circular silver sword, fist and wing of Airborne Forces.* b *Badge of the crack Legion Para regiment, the 1e REP — only the unit title changed when the 1e BEP was expanded, and this badge was worn from 1948 to 1961. In silver, it has green over red wings on each side of the numeral (J. P. Benavente).*

French Foreign Legion

cars and light tanks at Orange. The 2nd REI, partly a training formation and partly a combat unit, is on Corsica, as is the élite 2nd REP. The 3rd REI, after a number of years in Madagascar, is now in French Guiana. The 13th DBLE is at Djibouti in the former French Somaliland. A new regiment, the 5th RMP — 'Mixed

Sergeant of the 2e Regiment Etrangère Parachutiste *in the walking-out dress of the 1970s. The beltless tunic and trousers are khaki, the shoes black,' the shirt pale khaki and the tie grass-green. The képi is midnight blue, with a red top piped in the usual way with midnight blue. The gold grenade and gold false chin-strap are the only insignia. For parade purposes a black leather chin-strap is added and worn in the down position. Ranks below Senior Corporal wear the white képi at all times; ranks above only wear a white képi, for traditional reasons, when part of a colour party, but this is one of the many Legion practices which tends to vary from unit to unit and year to year. All non-commissioned ranks from Senior Corporal upwards wear a five-sided midnight blue collar tab bearing a gold grenade beneath three green soutaches; ranks below this grade wear instead a midnight blue diamond on the left upper arm bearing a green grenade and edged with triple green piping. The stiff midnight blue shoulder-boards bear the grenade beneath the three green soutaches for all ranks; the grenade is green up to Senior Corporal, gold above. The double gold chevrons of rank are worn here on a midnight blue patch, on both arms. The French paratrooper's qualification brevet — wings supporting a parachute above a star supported by two sprays of foliage — is worn above the right breast pocket; it is of silver, except for the foliate sprays, which are gold. The silver triangular* 2e REP *badge is worn on a leather fob from the same pocket. The crimson* fourragère *of the regiment's* Légion d'Honneur *is worn on the left* (Gerry Embleton).

The last twenty years

Regiment of the Pacific' — is based on the islands around Tahiti, as part of the facilities for the French nuclear test area; it is a technical and engineering unit. The paras of the 2nd REP saw action in the early 1970s in Chad, whose government evoked a defence agreement when threatened by internal troubles.

A sophisticated force of motorised and air-portable infantry, para-troopers, and light armour, the Legion retains its uniforms, its ceremonial, and its philosophy. Well paid, well fed, well equipped, and modern in every way that counts, it still embodies the fierce military pride of an earlier age. Men of all nationalities still serve under who-cares-what name, taking the second chance at life which the Legion offers them. It is still one of the toughest military units in the world, and since there are currently no wars to demand high manpower the Legion is able to be very selective in its recruiting. Only those who can meet the most exacting physical standards succeed in lasting out the three months of basic training required before posting to a regiment. The reputation of the Legion still attracts many officer applicants from other units, anxious to add a tour with this unique corps to their record — and it is still only the best of them who are accepted. Despite her love-hate relationship with the Legion over the decades, France knows she would be foolish to kill off this extraordinary survival of an age of hard-bitten mer-cenaries; in today's world it cannot be long before there is some more dirty, thankless fighting to be done, effi-ciently and without complaint — and the men who still present arms to Cap-tain Danjou's wooden hand every April 30 ask no more than that.

Modelling the Legion: the 1960s and 1970s

There are no commercial castings of légionnaires readily available in this country, although an American firm produces a 54 mm metal figure of a colonial paratrooper of a colour party which can easily be painted up as the 1st or 2nd REP. Modellers will not find it too demanding to produce figures using Airfix US or Australian infantry or figures in British battledress.

In action in Algeria the Legion wore green combat clothing with US style helmets, bush-hats, képis, or green berets depending upon the type of duty. Towards the end of the war the whole force was in French camouflage uniform. For parades the paras wear their camouflage suits with whitened webbing, sashes, decorations, and green berets. Other units wear a khaki battledress very similar to British 1949 pattern with a pale drill shirt and grass-green tie. The green epaulettes with red fringes are worn on the shoulders, the blue sash round the waist, and brown leather belts. Regi-mental badges are worn on the right breast hanging from a fob attached to the pocket button.

Many units wear coloured lanyards signifying that the regiment has been awarded a decoration as a whole — a French custom not followed in Britain. That of the 2nd REP, for instance, is the red lanyard of the *Légion d'Honneur,* and the 2nd REI wears the mixed red and pale blue of the Over-seas *Croix de Guerre.* The 3rd REI has the unique distinction of wearing a tri-ple lanyard, since it inherits the tradi-tions of the World War 1 and 2 RMLEs — the red *Légion d'Honneur,* the red and green 1914-18 *Croix de Guerre,* and the yellow and green *Médaille Militaire.* This latter is also worn by the 13th DBLE.

NCOs wear small reversed chevrons on both upper arms in green or gold, and all non-commissioned ranks wear a dark blue diamond-shaped patch on the left upper arm (immediately below any chevrons) bearing a green grenade in a triple green border; for sergeants and upwards the grenade is gold.